# CHILDREN'S

ROOMS

# CHILDREN'S

R O O M S

a mothercare book

## JANE LOTT

### PRENTICE HALL PRESS

New York  London  Toronto  Sydney  Tokyo

# CONTENTS

Prentice Hall Press
15 Columbus Circle
New York, NY 10023

Originally published in Great Britain by Conran Octopus Limited,
37 Shelton Street, London WC2H 9HN

PRENTICE HALL PRESS and colophon are registered trademarks of Simon & Schuster, Inc.

## DECORATING

*SECTION TWO: KNOW HOW*

## DECORATING TECHNIQUES

## FURNISHINGS AND FITTINGS

**Library of Congress Cataloging-in-Publication Data**

Lott, Jane
  Children's rooms.

  1. Children's rooms.   2. Interior decoration.
I. Title.
NK2117.C4L68   1990      747.7'7          89-22814
ISBN 0-13-132234-6

Printed in Hong Kong

10 9 8 7 6 5 4 3 2 1

First Prentice Hall Press Edition

# Introduction

What did your room mean to you as a child? What are your earliest memories of it? And do you remember what it looked like; the pattern on the wallpaper, or the way you could see a shelf of your favorite books when you lay in bed? Can you still conjure up the view from the window? And do you remember lying in bed and gazing at the walls, or making cracks or patches on the ceiling turn into human or animal shapes? Was your room a place you remember as a haven, your very own space – or was it your own but not your own, shared with a sister or brother? Was it somewhere you could feel at home, or just where you slept? Can you recall sitting with your friends whispering secrets or giggling manically together? Or quietly sitting with a favorite book or game?

Research in recent years has taught us much about the importance of environment. A child's home will affect his or her personality as well as their development. This does not mean a child will suffer unless he has a whole suite of grand rooms at his disposal. But it is important for a child's sense of well-being and confidence that some care and attention is paid to his home. If a space has been specially designed for the child to sleep, play and work in, then he will do all these things more satisfactorily.

## Planning through the years

Most parents start off with the best of intentions at the outset. Planning and decorating a baby's room is a thrilling idea; one of the pleasures of having children. Pregnant women and expectant fathers fill in the waiting days picking wallpaper and contemplating cribs, and everybody smiles fondly, spotting the nesting instinct at work. But as the first baby grows into a toddler and beyond, life rushes on, there is work to do, another baby on the way or arrived, holidays to plan, hobbies to catch up on and a child to pick up from playgroup or school. Suddenly you may realize with

a shock that the wallpaper the toddler has been carefully peeling from the walls for the past week or two is the same scene of picnicking rabbits you selected seven years ago. Not only does your eldest think it pretty soppy, but he hasn't got anywhere except the bedroom floor to do his homework or build his construction set, which is why it keeps getting stepped on and why he keeps yelling at his little brother. Toys are everywhere, quite a few are broken, and he can never find his bedroom slippers, which is why it hurt when he stubbed his toe this morning.

A scenario such as this demonstrates the continuing importance of planning for different ages and stages of maturity, and of always thinking of the child's future as well as present needs and tastes. The book's second chapter, Ages and Stages, helps you to look ahead to the next stage when equipping and decorating a child's room.

A well-planned child's room won't only be good for your son or daughter, it will make a big difference to your life too. If you know that older children are happily and safely playing or working upstairs, in their rooms, you can get on confidently with your own projects for a while. They may be content to stay in their own room and play or read on waking up in the morning, rather than bursting in on you at dawn or sneaking down to the television set. They will be more ready to go to bed when they are tired if they feel relaxed and at home in their room. Friends will want to come and play, and perhaps stay overnight, because they too feel comfortable in the room, and there's lots to do.

There is far less friction in a house when everybody has some space of their own. If your child has a particular interest, he will be able to develop it in his own room, secure in the knowledge that his model or construction won't be disrupted because you have had to clear the only table in the house for supper. You won't be angry because

there is a "mess" somewhere – which seems especially unfair when that "mess" represents something your child is trying to do. You won't stifle the child's endeavor and he won't get in your way either.

It is also important for children to learn to look after things, to take some responsibility in however small a way. Where better to start than in their own homes, looking after their room and their possessions? "A place for everything and everything in its place" needn't be a bossy and old-fashioned formula. If it means that all the pieces of the jigsaw puzzle are back in the box for next time and the tiny pieces of model airplane haven't been vacuumed up off the carpet because they have their own storage box or boxes, children will eventually appreciate the point of keeping order.

## The role of a child's room

One of the most essential functions of a child's bedroom is to be a refuge. No child has ever grown up without experiencing frustration, anger or disappointment at some stage. Small setbacks can seem very large indeed to someone under ten years of age and a spell of time in a pleasant bedroom generally soothes a child wonderfully after a quarrel with a friend, or some failure or frustration they have experienced. Of course this need will not arise until children are a long way past the nursery stage, but before then there will be many occasions when their room needs to be a refuge and a haven: when a child is feeling unwell; or at the end of a long, tiring day when to be tucked in and kissed good night in his own safe and familiar room is just what is needed.

There are many ways in which you

*The ideal children's room is one in which they are happy to play, work and pursue their hobbies – as well as sleep. It will be a haven for them and an exciting place to which they can invite friends.*

can make your child's room special, besides decorating and furnishing it with his tastes and needs in mind. Reading a bedtime story to him in bed every night will make him look forward to bedtime. His own tape cassette player and a small selection of music and story cassette tapes provides another pleasure to anticipate at bedtime and first thing in the morning before his parents wake up. And putting the odd treat in the bedroom to surprise him will also help make a child feel that his room is indeed a special and a happy place.

## A home for children

A child's room is not, of course, his whole life, and you should not expect it to be somewhere he spends his days, only appearing for meals and trips to school. Children are in and out of their rooms like jack-in-the-boxes. A young baby will naturally spend a considerable part of the day, as well as the night, in the nursery – not only sleeping but often being fed, changed and simply cuddled there. As the baby gets older, and sleeps less, he will want to sit and play wherever you are. Later on he will crawl, stagger or walk around as much of the house as he is allowed access to. Under the age of three, in fact, children rarely play on their own for very long, so they won't spend much time in their room when they are this young. They want and need adults in the background, quite often in the foreground, and they will occupy themselves wherever their caregivers are, because this is where they feel safe. As if by instinct they

# Introduction

*Christmas is an exciting festival for all children, and if you can help an older child to decorate her room in a seasonal way it will seem even more special at this time.*

know that they will find their opportunities to learn, and to expand their range of abilities by copying adults. Copying speech, and copying actions such as washing vegetables, sweeping floors, putting things into and taking them out of cupboards, "just like" grown ups do is all part of their development. They need to be able to tug at a parent, to ask mommy or daddy to read a book, to help them with a puzzle, or find a pencil and some paper.

It is important in any case that children share the whole house with you. You didn't have children in order to push them away: you like to know something about what they're up to, to chat with them, to do things together and meet their friends. You simply need to plan a little so that other parts of the house have something to offer children and are safe for them too. The first chapter of this book, Around the House, looks at all the areas children use, room by room, and considers how they can be made both appropriate to children's needs and safe.

In time, however, you will find that your children enjoy their room for longer stretches during the day. Suddenly one day you may be aware that all is silence and so, fearing the worst, you creep upstairs. Your child is in his room, quietly pursuing some occupation with great concentration, and you realize that he has reached a new stage. And when a friend comes, they vanish up there immediately. You know that, since time began, children have enjoyed their private life together, out of the earshot of adults, playing fantasy games, making secret clubs, forming gangs and chattering away. Home is important as a place outside school where children can cement

friendships. And since it would be unrealistic to think that adults never need a break from children's company, particularly in smaller houses and apartments, it is also true to say that ensuring that children have a place of their own to go to has certainly helped parents, too.

In the following pages there are ideas and guidance about all aspects of planning, furnishing and decorating children's rooms. Section One, entitled "Ideas," will give you plenty of suggestions for furnishing and equipping a child's room through all the different stages up to the age of about ten. Shared as well as single rooms are discussed. Practical choices of lighting, wall and window coverings, flooring and heating are all discussed, with both safety and suitability in mind.

The chapter on decorating different children's rooms will inspire parents with ideas for their baby's, toddler's, pre-school and older child's or children's rooms.

Section Two of the book, entitled "Know how," gives practical information to help you implement the ideas in Section One, to decorate and furnish a child's room yourself. From painting and wallpapering to making the blinds and cushions, doing it yourself will enable you to create a room for your child that is both personal and unique.

Family rooms may be fancier these days, and kitchens more expensive, but no other room in the house will ever have as much special character, or offer as much comfort and sheer delight, as a well-planned child's room.

# IDEAS

# A R O U N D
# THE HOUSE

Children live in their home – all of it. Babies are not in the
nursery every moment; toddlers don't occupy themselves quietly
in their own rooms all morning. Even older children are in and
out of the kitchen, living room and the yard as well as their own
rooms. At all ages, children use and enjoy their home to its full
extent. At the same time, they need their own personal space, a
room with its own character, where they feel they belong.

# Your child's space

It is important to anticipate the arrival of your first child and to prepare your home for its new inhabitant. Otherwise you will find that you are either cross or anxious and he is frustrated for much of the time. Life will run much more smoothly if you take some time to organize how your child or children will fit into your everyday life, both safely and happily.

## Children's bedroom

Think about: sleep, storage, play space, safety. This room is the basic building block, where your child will spend a lot of time and where most of his possessions will be kept. This is where many of a young baby's and older child's routines will take place, from diaper changing, possibly bathing and feeding, to bedtime stories, dressing and undressing, as well as playing, reading, working and entertaining friends.

## Bathroom

Think about: safe storage, bath safety. Medicines and other substances that are dangerous and bottles that can break will need to be kept in a childproof lockable cupboard, out of a child's reach. Babies will usually be bathed in a separate bath, on a firm stand. When they graduate to the big bath, you may want to use a safety mat. Diaper changing and undressing may take place here. A stepstool may be handy to help an older child reach the wash basin. If the bathroom gets crowded in the morning, you might consider having water plumbed into one or more bedrooms.

## Parents' bedroom

Think about: new baby, children's visits. You may give a newborn baby a temporary home here, and he will need a sleeping and storage corner. Older children may come in at night for extra reassurance, while visiting mom and dad in the morning is an important ritual for many families: you may keep a few books or toys near the bed.

## Stairs

Think about: safety. For younger children, you should initially fit a baby gate, as well as taking the time to teach them how to come up and down stairs safely, always supervising them until they are completely confident on their own. Stairs should be well-lit and toys should never be left on them.

## Hall or foyer

Think about: storage. This is often a good place to keep children's outdoor clothes, shoes and boots, as well as a baby's traveling bag and older children's ready-packed swimming or gym bag, etc., ready for quick getaways. Low pegs (better staggered than in a row) or a low coatstand will enable children to hang up and store their own possessions. Depending on the space, the stroller or carriage and children's tricycles or bicycles may be kept here.

## Kitchen

Think about: safety, play space, eating. Breakable bottles and jars, as well as toxic materials such as bleach, must be locked away, out of a child's reach. Babies and toddlers may want to be with you, but they need to be kept away from heat sources, machines and knives. The kitchen is a good place for messy play and helping.

## Living room

Think about: safety, play space, adult life, storage. Some people prefer to keep this a child-free zone: fine, if provision has been made elsewhere. Most parents at least prefer the children not to "spread" all over the living room: this will be easier to control if they have their own allocated storage. Children may like their own-sized chairs or seats for when they are there with you, or watching television. Any fires must be guarded at all times (see page 22).

## Playroom

Think about: safety, durability, storage. If your children are lucky enough to have a separate playroom it will need to be robust and safe. Choose non-slip, durable flooring; furniture and equipment need not be new or smart but must be stable. Plan for lots of storage.

## Outside areas

Think about: safe play equipment and some level hard surfacing. Jungle gyms, swings and slides should be on grass, but children will need a path or terrace on which to roller skate, play ball games and ride tricycles. Make sure it is swept regularly to remove leaves and debris, or it becomes dangerously slippery when wet.

*Up and down, in and out: children don't stand still but move all over the house. Each room needs to adapt.*

# The kitchen

The kitchen is often the hub of the house, and from a very early age children will like to be there with you. As babies, they will be entertained by watching you as you wash vegetables or cook, and you can smile or talk and sing to them as you do it. Later, they will enjoy being given small helping tasks to do, such as stirring a cake mix. Of course, young children may make a mess, but the more they help the better they will get at it. And if any room in the house is easy to clean up, it ought to be the kitchen.

## Play

The kitchen is usually the most suitable room for rolling out pastry or playing with playdough, for mixing paints or other messy play. Many kitchens have a suitable large table, which can always be covered with newspaper or a plastic cloth. And if you have to be in the kitchen anyway, you won't have to take time off from what you are doing to supervise this kind of activity. You might keep a child's washable plastic overall or apron on a low peg or in a kitchen drawer for this kind of play.

## Eating

Children usually eat in the kitchen, so you will need to think about where they will sit. A baby who cannot sit unaided, but who is starting to be given tastes of a few solid foods, may try these out sitting on your lap. When this is not convenient, or becomes too messy, he can sit on the floor in a low chair with a reclining back and a washable tray.

An older child will sit in a highchair for meals. Some highchairs convert into a low chair and table: you may find these very useful, as they double as safe-height play tables. Toddlers who want to sit in an ordinary chair but are too small to reach the table can sit in a high chair without a tray pushed right up to the table, delivering them to their food at a convenient height. Alternatively, you could attach a clip-on child seat to your table, or use a box seat on top of an ordinary chair.

Once your children are old enough to sit on adult dining chairs, bear in mind that upholstered fabric seats are best avoided unless you want to be scrubbing off ground-in bits of food and sour milk every other day. Washable plasticized fabric is easy to wipe clean if you have chairs with upholstered seats. You can re-cover removable fabric seats quite easily by removing the tacks and taking off the old fabric, and then using tacks or a staple gun to attach the new fabric, stretching it tightly over the seat, especially at the corners.

Because children often finish eating before adults, you may be happy for them to get down and play while you finish, providing you can still keep a careful eye on them. For younger children it will be a good idea to keep a few toys in the kitchen, perhaps stored in a toy box under a table, or in a low cupboard. Kitchen utensils themselves are regarded by children as wonderful toys, of course; you will need to put breakable china, sharp knives and food

*Above A toy box in the kitchen will usually enable a young child to amuse himself for a short time while you are cooking. The kitchen is a good place for painting and messy play too – it can be cleaned up easily.*

*Left This clever foldaway shelf in a corner of the kitchen, plus suitably low chair, means that a child can be with you, but not in your way. A low table is a good alternative.*

packets and jars out of reach, storing only items like saucepans in the lower cupboards.

## Safety precautions

The kitchen may be a convenient place for a young child to be, but it is not necessarily safe – and you may find a baby on the loose wildly irritating when you are trying to cook in a hurry. Many parents use a playpen in the kitchen. Though it is not a good idea for the

baby to be in it all the time, it may be extremely useful if you leave the room for a few minutes to answer the doorbell or go to the bathroom. Whether there is a playpen or not, you should make sure the baby's area of the kitchen is well away from the stove and out of the main circulation space, where hot food may be carried from the stove to the table, or where the baby or his playpen would be always under people's feet.

■ See pages 22-23 *for Planning for safety*

# The living room

From the start, your baby will come in here to be with the family when it is gathered together, and to meet visitors. Initially he will probably be in a port-a-crib or bassinet, or being passed from lap to lap, but later he will want to play a more active role. As children grow older, they won't stay neatly on a rug waving a rattle, but will demand much more from the living room, including scrambling all over the best furniture.

Every family makes its own rules about what is permissible, and banning children altogether from the "grown ups'" room is only practical if there is another room for them to go to. Most parents reach a working compromise that takes into account that the living room is the "best" room in the house. For example, it is simplest to ban drinks in the living room if spilling apple juice is going to spoil the sofa or the carpet, as well as upset you. Keep only those toys in the living room that you expect to be played with there. Even if you don't mind children turning the sofa into a ship or chairs into a den, do insist that they remove their shoes first – socks or bare feet will wear and dirty the upholstery fabric far less.

### The young baby
A good living room idea for small babies is a portable mobile-carrier, which can follow the baby around without being on view the whole time. The most usual design is a bent arm, which can be clamped to the edge of a table or chair, from which a small mobile, or a small, soft swinging toy, can be suspended. An alternative is to use a coat hanger, to which small soft toys or pretty pieces of paper are tied, and suspend this or hook it on to a chair back or table edge, out of a baby's reach.

A sturdy, attractive rug or throw can live on the arm or back of a chair or sofa, ready to go on the floor for the baby. It should not be too fragile, nor should it shed – young children put everything in their mouths and can choke on fragments of fabric. When your baby is six weeks old or so, he can be put on the floor in a "bouncing cradle." This is a comfortable and useful vantage point from which to watch the world or play with a toy stretched across the frame.

### Toy storage
Most parents like to keep some toys in the living room for when the baby or child is around. They could, of course, be stored in the child's bedroom and be transported in a carrying box or basket, but it may be just as easy to store them in the living room itself if there is space. They could unobtrusively occupy a shelf or two in a cupboard or a drawer in a desk, or you could devote a low bookcase, storage unit or alcove cupboard to children's items. A second coffee table with a lower shelf or one built on the hollow cube principle may be a good idea too: it looks like normal furniture, but can be used both to store toys and games and as a surface for playing.

Alternatively you could use a pretty basket for toys (such as a wicker shopping basket, a log basket or laundry basket) or an actual toy box. Straw baskets can be painted or sprayed with non-toxic, oil-based paints to make them blend in with your color scheme if you intend them to stay in the living room for some time.

It is tempting to simply throw all the toys in after use, but do try to have a sort-out at least once a week as soon as the kind of toy changes from simple rattles to toys with pieces. The appearance of orderly toy boxes will complement the look of your living room, while a jumble of children's odds and ends will not.

You may deliberately choose to keep some toys in the living room precisely because they are special – a doll's house, perhaps, particularly if it is a family heirloom, or other toys from your own childhood which you have saved, such as a Noah's ark with animals, china dolls or old windup toys. These will look attractive on display, and it will be exciting for the children to be allowed to play with them on special occasions when you are all together.

### Furnishing and seating
Think ahead about maintenance and safety in the living room. Loose covers that can be washed are more practical than permanent, non-washable upholstery, for example. Until the children are older, keep precious ornaments up high and the liquor cabinet locked. Don't put pretty vases on small, unstable surfaces, and never leave packs of cigarettes and matches where they can be reached.

Children will probably watch television in the family living room which enables you to keep an eye on what they are watching, and to watch with them from time to time. To stop children living too close to the television (which emits a certain amount of low-level radiation) you could place some child-sized chairs at a reasonable distance; they can also be used for games, and for playing or drawing at a low table. If you have a video, you may find a video guard a good idea; it prevents the buttons being fiddled with.

*Children's special possessions, such as this doll's house, can fit well into a "grown-up" room, as can a small table and chair for quiet play.*

# The playroom

*A comfortable, well-planned playroom is one in which adults would be happy to sit as well as young children to play. The use of brightly colored fabric, wood and basketwork add to the room's appeal and its versatility. The day bed means that this room could also be used to accommodate occasional visitors overnight.*

If you have the space and/or several children, a separate playroom will be a godsend, particularly if the children have shared or small bedrooms. A playroom doesn't necessarily have to be exclusively children's territory: it could double as an extra family room, a sewing or hobbies room, or even as the family eating room, if the kitchen is small.

The use of the room could alter with the changing requirements of the family as the children grow. For very young children, the room needs to be a safe place to play, preferably close at hand to the kitchen, where you will be most of the time, and where messy activities like painting, modelling or cutting out can take place without fuss. The playroom should be a place where

toys or games can be left out, if the children want to go on with the same activities the next day. Children could even have some of their meals here.

As the children grow older, the playroom might adapt to take a television or video and space-consuming activities such as a ping-pong table, miniature billiards, a doll's house and so on. Gradually, it will grow into the "den," or rumpus room, of teenagers, a social center with music and perhaps hobby equipment. If children of different ages share a bedroom, they will appreciate an extra place to work quietly.

You may not think you have space for a separate playroom, but a playroom can be made from a cellar or attic conversion, and would be well

■ See pages 50-51 *for different types of flooring*

worthwhile in terms of the pressure it removes from the rest of the house. Some people give over a little-used formal dining room to children and adapt the kitchen or living room for eating instead, or they manage, by clever use of storage, to combine dining room and playroom.

It is often a temptation to fill such a room with old or junk furniture, and there is nothing wrong with this, provided the old furniture is neither precarious nor damaged. It could all be painted one color, or a mixture of cheerful colors, or stripped and stencilled, to make it look more homogenous. Beware of sofas or chairs that need re-upholstering: the children may think it a great game to pull them completely to pieces.

## Practical matters

There are some important considerations in a playroom which don't necessarily apply to children's bedrooms. These include:

*Flooring* This should be sturdy and practical. Good choices for younger children are: wood, cork tiles, cushioned vinyl or linoleum, good quality, smooth-surfaced matting, rubber, or easy cleaning low-pile carpet tiles. Older children might find a carpet more congenial, but long-pile carpet should still be avoided as it will be subject to attack from crumbs, spilled drinks, glue and paint. A rug could be added to a hard floor, but must be firmly fixed to it.

*Storage* Adequate storage is essential and could take the form of fixed shelving or a reasonable sized basic bookcase, a chest with deep drawers, a dresser with a cupboard and shelves, a tall cupboard with deep shelves or a toy chest. One or more of these will be necessary for books, games, drawing equipment, records, tapes and whatever else your children grow into. It might be backed up with stacking crates, work baskets or a filing cabinet.

If the playroom doubles as a breakfast room or family dining room,

you will need a separate cupboard for cereals, china, glass and cutlery.

*Work surface* A stable surface for cards, games and hobbies, as well as homework, will be needed. This might be a built-in work unit, a central circular table, a folding or expanding table, or a desk. A washable surface would obviously be sensible, but a handsome table could be protected with the addition of felt undercloth and a washable vinyl overcloth. It is advisable to tape a cloth down if there are toddlers about who might give it a good tug.

*Seating* Straight-backed chairs would be needed for working and eating at table. For more relaxed seating, provide a sofa, some cheap upholstered chairs, large floor cushions or bean bags. In some playrooms, a seating platform could be

*An attic conversion, with solid wood block floor and ample storage, has enabled this playroom to be created.*

made from cheap wood, painted and covered with carpet or made comfortable with the addition of cushions. Younger children could have small seats and a table, or stools.

*Lighting* A good overhead light or bright wall lighting will be needed, plus stable task lighting such as an angled desk lamp. Avoid floor lamps, as they are likely to be knocked over.

*Electric outlets* Install too many rather than too few, and position one or two midway up a wall, where equipment that will sit on a work surface or table can be plugged in without danger of trailing wires. Outlets not in use should be fitted with a cover.

■ See pages 118-123 *for building your own shelves*

# Outside areas

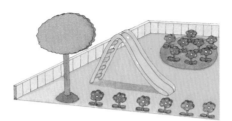

If it can be managed, some sort of outside space accessible directly from the home gives a marvelous dimension to a child's life. Here children can safely let off steam, gain exercise, indulge in messy play and learn how things grow. Not everybody has a yard, of course, but a patio or a balcony or roof terrace (if these last two can be made safe) can also provide such opportunities.

If your outside space is small, consider paving it rather than having a pocket handkerchief lawn. The grass will be battered by children and turn into wet slippery mud after rain; from the children's point of view it is better to have firm, attractive paving for tricycles, scooters, ball games and general running about. A sand box can be set into paving and plants can be grown in the gaps between stones. Gravel is not good for children: they will throw it, bring it into the house, and it is hard to ride across it.

A balcony or roof terrace must have a surrounding wall or fence at least 3ft (90cm) high, with no gaps or footholds for climbing over. Trellis fencing, or open railings, for example, would be too dangerous, and would need to be backed or covered either with solid hardboard or wood, with plexiglass or other solid plastic sheeting, or with strong, fine-mesh wire netting. Anything lower than 3ft (90cm) should be extended upwards, again with strong and solid material. Do not leave anything near a fence or wall that a child could use as a climbing block, such as a plant tub or garden seat. If you are not happy about the safety of a balcony or roof terrace, keep the entrance to it locked and hide the key.

### Playing in the yard

The kind of activities children enjoy outdoors, which would be less easy to set up in their own rooms, include sand play, water play, gardening, climbing, riding on wheeled toys and playing running and jumping games. An ideal yard for a child would include some of the following:

*A sand box* A lid should be placed over the sand whenever it is not in use, both to stop it becoming soaked by rain, and to prevent local animals from continually using it.

*A wading pool* Life is easier if you have an outside tap for filling it.

*A jungle gym* or some other activity equipment such as a swing, slide, rope ladder, bouncer or trampoline. These will be possible only if a garden is reasonably spacious and should preferably be placed on a grassed area

or other safety surfacing. Make sure that swings, slides and jungle gyms are firmly anchored in the ground, and that small children playing on them are supervised by an adult at all times.

*A tree house, tent or wigwam.*

*Wheeled toys* These may take the form of a tricycle, bicycle, scooter, roller skates or pedal car, depending on the child's age.

*Bat and ball games* These will depend

**Above** *A shed can be turned into a useful outdoor play house for young children.*

**Left** *A shaded patio is an ideal place for a sand box (sand can be swept up easily) and for riding wheeled toys.*

on the size of the yard. While a large area would be needed for a real game of tennis, other ball games, using for example plastic racquets and a sponge ball, should be possible in most yards. There is also tetherball, which one or two children can play, batting a ball attached to a central pole. You may want to ban baseball unless your yard is vast, or at least restrict games to a hard-surfaced area.

Not many children will be lucky enough to have the whole of this grand list, and of course there are public parks, playgrounds, sports centers, playgroups and woodland where they can enjoy more physical play. But having a few of these items in the yard will mean hours of entertainment without having to travel away from home. They don't have to be costly – a sand box can be a hole in the ground

lined with wood, or a plastic box; the old baby bath will do for water play; washed yogurt and other food pots and kitchen spoons are fine for digging and castle-making. A giant cardboard box from a local shop could be turned into a temporary play house, and a sheet over a drying rack or two deck chairs makes a good tent. Children love improvising.

Children also enjoy working in a yard, learning to tell the difference between weeds and flowers, helping with the raking of leaves and other yard jobs. They can be given a small plot of their own where they can plant quick-growing and easy vegetables such as carrots and green beans (radishes are even easier, but not many children like the taste) and simple annual flowers can be grown from seed.

Observing and even collecting wildlife, and keeping a bird feeder are activities which can easily be encouraged. A basic bird feeder can be made by nailing a flat board to a pole high enough to prevent cats jumping on it, and knocking it into the ground; or you could use half-coconuts hung from a tree branch.

# Planning for safety

Until you have children, it is hard to anticipate what will be a danger to them, but anticipate you must. Use this checklist and ask someone who does have experience of children to walk around your home with you. They will be like a kind of geiger counter, set off at the sight of trailing cords and unguarded fires.

Always look for household goods which meet or exceed current child safety standards. Ask your pediatrician about safety guidelines and regulations for toys, appliances, car seats, and other items. You may also call or write to your local U.S. Consumer Product Safety Commission.

## Fire

Fire is the most common cause of accidental death in the home for children, and many die from breathing in noxious fumes or from suffocation rather than from burning.

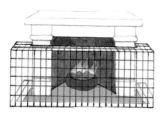

*Smoke detectors* These can be battery operated or hard wired, and both are reasonably priced. The battery type is cheaper and easier to install, but you must remember to check the battery and change it when it runs out. The best place in the home to install one is generally at the top of the stairwell (smoke rises) or

outside the kitchen door – you want it to be triggered by a real fire, but not every time you turn the stove on. Push the test button regularly to make sure that the alarm is still working properly.

*Fireguards* A free-standing mesh spark guard is useful to stop any flying sparks from an open fire but is not sufficient on its own. Use it inside a proper nursery floor-standing fireguard, which has a top as well as sides and stands at least 8in (20cm) from the heat source; this can be used with all kinds of fires and heaters. It must be securely fixed to the wall with the special clip fitting provided: you will have to drill two holes in the wall to fix these. If your heater is wall mounted too high for a free-standing guard, buy a wall-mounted one. It will have a panel that opens to enable you to work the heater's controls. (See page 54 for more on heating.)

Never put anything on top of a fireguard, wet washing included, and never allow your children to climb on it.
*Fire blankets* These are useful in the case of small or kitchen fires. They should be at least 36in (90cm) square, and not kept too near the cooktop – you don't want to reach over the fire in order to get at the fire blanket.
*Furniture* Look for combustion modified (CM) foam for upholstered furniture. Polyurethane foam upholstery gives off toxic fumes when it burns, which it does very quickly.

This filling is now banned in several countries, and if you already have some in your home you may wish to replace it.

## In the kitchen
*Child-resistant catches*
These cheap, handy little items can be screwed on to the inside of your cupboard doors, and will make it more difficult for a baby or toddler to open them. However, they cannot be fitted to all types of cupboard, and it may be difficult to make them stiff enough to prevent children opening them, but just loose enough for you to manage. Some children

regard them as challenges and bang and bang away until they snap them.

It is best to regard these catches as an aid rather than a failsafe, and to store dangerous materials such as oven cleaner, bleach and disinfectant in a high cupboard or a locked one (with the key stored separately elsewhere, out of a child's reach).
*Child-resistant refrigerator lock* It is usually exasperating rather than dangerous when a child raids the refrigerator, but he might get hold of an opened bottle of wine, or some medicine that has to be kept cold. A refrigerator lock will at least lessen such hazardous risks.

## Stairs
Train your baby to go up and down stairs safely (crawling up, coming down backwards on his tummy) but meanwhile prevent access to the stairs.
*Baby gates* These are made of wood or metal and are screwed to the wall, but they open and shut easily to let

older members of the family through. Some models have a "walk-through" middle section. They are of use at the top or bottom of stairs and at the door to rooms you do not want a child to enter, such as the bathroom or workroom. The U.S. Consumer Product Commission recommends that you choose a style of gate other than the accordion-type. Gates with a straight top edge and rigid mesh screen are safer.
*Baby barriers:* The better kind come with cups that are fixed to the wall and take the extendable arms of the barrier, which means that it can be moved around the house. Another type relies on pressure from extendable

arms ending in rubber buffers to keep the barrier in place and can be dislodged if a child shakes it violently. Do not set up a barrier with a space of more than 2in (5cm) beneath it: a baby might try and wriggle beneath this.

## Bathroom

*Non-slip bath mats* These help to prevent a small child from slipping, though children should always be supervised in the bath.

*Medicine cabinet* Medicines

must be stored in a childproof cabinet. If it is a locked one, hide the key.

## Windows and doors

*Safety glass* French windows, picture windows, or any fully glazed doors are potentially dangerous. Small children can trip and crash

through a glass door or simply forget that the glass is there.

The best type of safety glass is laminated glass, made from two sheets of ordinary glass with a sheet of plastic permanently bonded between them. If the glass breaks, it stays in one piece, held together by the plastic layer. This type of safety glass is quite expensive.

Tempered glass is heat-treated so that it shatters into small rounded pieces which are considerably less harmful than jagged splinters.

Wire glass is not a safety glass as such, but the wire does help to hold the glass together if it should break, and also makes it more visible.

*Safety film* This clear

polyester plastic comes in rolls which you apply yourself. It holds broken glass in place but will only work properly on glass with one side that is completely flat, not on uneven, patterned glass. Once in place, it cannot be removed.

*Window locks* You can buy casement window locks which prevent the window being opened enough to let a child through. For sash windows, a burglar-proof lock prevents the window being opened more than 4in (10cm). Pivoted windows can also be fitted with a lock that restricts the opening.

*Automatic door closers* These screw on to the top of the frame of interior doors and stop the door from slamming shut. This prevents a child's fingers being pinched at either the hinge side or the lock side.

## Around the house

*Outlet guards* These inexpensive plastic outlet covers plug into standard electric outlets and prevent children poking anything into an empty outlet, or

trying to plug in an electrical item. Remember to replace them after using the outlet. If you have old-style non-shuttered electric outlets, these should be replaced.

*Corner cushions* These are useful for covering the sharp corners of all those items which small children seem to run straight into – tables, low-units and protruding shelves especially. One of the commonest causes of home accidents is children bumping their heads on radiators, and a home-made corner cushion may help. For more information about home safety contact: The U.S. Product Safety Commission, Washington, D.C. 20207.

---

## SAFETY ALL DAY

| ◤ MORNING | ◥ DAY | ◣ EVENING | ● GENERAL |
|---|---|---|---|
| ■ **Stove and cooktop guards:** *A stove guard fits on to most stoves that have a back panel; a cooktop guard modifies a cooktop set into a countertop.*<br>■ **Curly cord:** *Useful for kettles and other apparatus to avoid trailing cord.* | ■ **Playpen:** *If you are worried about a child underfoot while cooking, use a playpen. Put the baby in it from an early age to get used to the idea.*<br>■ **Safety harnesses:** *Besides its outdoor uses, you should use a safety harness in the highchair.* | ■ **Baby monitor:** *Unless you can hear your baby crying from anywhere in the house, a baby monitor is a great boon.*<br>■ **Bed guard:** *This helps your child get used to his first proper bed.*<br>■ **Night light:** *A small glow at night is reassuring.* | ■ **Video guard:** *This control panel cover will stop children fiddling with the video controls.*<br>■ **Heaters:** *Before investing in heating units or systems, check their safety with your local U.S. Consumer Product Safety Commission.* |

# AGES AND STAGES

In the same way that babies and children grow out of clothes and equipment, they also outgrow stages in their lives and move on to new ones. This may happen gradually, over a few months or weeks, or it can take place apparently overnight, but either way you have to react to it.

Some furniture can simply be adapted and can stay usefully in your home for years, while other items have a shorter life. A room, however, should need only minor adjustments to modify it as a child grows older, if you think ahead. In this chapter we look at how a child's needs change, and what you might do to accommodate this change painlessly.

# Choosing the room

If your child's room could be one of a number in the house, think about various factors before you make a choice. A tiny baby may not need more than a cubbyhole, but an older child, or children sharing a room, will need more space. It might even be worth allocating the largest bedroom in a house to children, and the parents having a smaller one. The benefits will be felt in less clutter elsewhere in the house, room for them to play without tripping over each other and quarrelling, and not having to be unremittingly tidy.

If the house has three or more storeys, the advantages of putting children on the top floor are that you will be insulated from their noise, they will feel more private and, when they are older, it will be mainly them, not you, who has to do the climbing. The disadvantages are that a sick child, or one who is scared in the night, will feel isolated, and babies and sick children will require constant trips up and down stairs. Young children will find it a great trek up to and down from their rooms, increasing the danger of their stumbling on the stairs.

Attic rooms often have low walls and an interesting shape and can make charming children's rooms. Bear in mind, however, that rooms in the roof tend to be cold in winter and hot in summer, so they may not be very practical unless you can insulate them.

## Noise

If young children are too close to a noisy living room, they may find it hard to sleep, so choosing a bedroom directly over a room where loud music or late-night television dominates may be a mistake unless you muffle their floor with carpetpad and carpet. The same goes for a room overlooking a noisy street. On the other hand, giving them the quietest spot in the house may habituate them to only being able to sleep in silent surroundings, which could be a problem in later life. If their room overlooks a street with bright

street lamps, blackout curtains will help and thick ones will keep out some noise at the same time.

You may feel more secure if a baby sleeps in a room adjoining yours, yet be happier if older children are further away from your bedroom, both for the sake of your own privacy and so that their noise doesn't necessarily wake you at the same time as they wake up.

## Which way does it face?

Think about the orientation of a room. Obviously, most people prefer a light and sunny room, but this will be of more relevance to children, who spend time in their own room in the day, than to adults who just go there to sleep. An east-facing room into which the sun pours early in the morning will need thick or dark-lined window coverings if children are not to be woken up very early. You may find that a west-facing room overheats in the evening on a hot day if the windows, conforming to safety measures, cannot be opened very wide. Thin blinds may be useful in such a room to cut out the strongest sun while still allowing light through.

A north-facing room usually has a good quality of light, but only if the windows are large. Otherwise it will be on the dark side, and probably rather chilly too. Fortunately, there are ways to compensate, with cheerful colors and good lighting. The same goes for a directly east-facing room, from which the sun moves away, usually by mid-morning at the latest. South- and west-facing rooms generally have the most attractive overall orientation, but waking up to a sunny east-facing room makes for a cheerful start to the day.

## The condition of the room

Other factors which might influence your choice are the room's existing state of repair, the amount and kind of storage already there, the shape of the room, and any special features.

If the room is in a bad condition, you will have to deal with the underlying reasons for this before you can

progress with decoration. There is no point in trying to cover up the bad state of repair. Quite apart from the fact that the decoration will not look good for long, a room that is damp or has other fundamental problems will be bad for a child's health.

However, there are benefits in planning a room from scratch: you are not constrained by the way things are. If money allows, you can lay a new floor, plan plenty of storage, perhaps even alter ugly features or enlarge a window. Think through your options in terms of your day-to-day routine and

your budget, and try to anticipate what your child's needs might be, a few years hence.

Even if the room is basically sound, and you are not carrying out major work, you may not need to be totally limited by the way it is at the moment. It may be well worth enduring extra work and planning now to make the room much more pleasant, practical and timesaving in years to come.

Would it make sense to move a radiator in order to free a wall for a full-length bookcase? Would you rather have floor-to-ceiling shelving than the existing alcove cupboard? Perhaps you would really prefer to have stripped wood flooring than the patterned carpet that is now laid on the floor. Are there enough electric outlets, and in useful enough positions? Could the lighting be better arranged, with wall lights as well as, or instead of, an overhead fixture? Try and work out what would be ideal, and then see how far the room can in fact be altered.

Plumbing is relevant at this stage if you are thinking of installing a water supply to the room, or to a new small bathroom next door. The advantages of having water in the room are many: it is extremely convenient when babies are small for sponge bathing, changing the baby's diaper, and quick rinses of clothing or bedding, and will continue to take the pressure off the family bathroom in coming years. The only disadvantages are the danger of a child causing a flood or leaving the hot tap endlessly running. But the luxury of a children's bathroom will not only reduce the line for the main bathroom but will mean that adult baths won't be full of plastic boats, bunny rabbit soaps and wet towels now, and full of teenagers in fifteen years' time.

If money is limited, there are two approaches. One is to work around what is there, which is often the only option, especially in rented accommodation. The alternative approach is to spend money now on structural alterations and wait a while before decorating. Provided the room itself is warm and clean, there are some advantages to having a bare room from a child's point of view. Bare walls can be temporarily decorated by the children themselves, or can have a mural or blackboard paint applied. Babies only notice their immediate surroundings, and you can hang as many interesting mobiles near their crib in a bare room as in a finished one.

However, children must not sleep or play in a room which has had treatment for woodworm, dry rot or other infestation recently carried out, until a safe period of time has elapsed. Nor should they sleep or play in a room while decorating is going on – paint and other fumes may be bad for them. Try to get any treatments or decorating done before children take possession of the room, or move them out temporarily while decorating.

*A wonderfully vast children's room can be made from an attic area, and the space will be especially welcome where children are sharing.*

■ See pages 98-115 *for decorating techniques*

# Choosing a bed

You need to think about beds for children in two stages. The first bed, for a baby, can initially take the form of a cradle, port-a-crib or bassinet, before a full-sized crib is needed. The options for the second bed are many, but partly depend on the size of the bedroom, and whether or not two children are sharing it.

**Bassinet** A bassinet can be both charming and practical. It is lightweight and snug, and is useful for carrying the new baby around your home as well as for keeping close to your bed at night. It can rest on a special stand or on the floor, provided it is not dusty, and there is no danger from pets or older children. It cannot however be used to transport your baby in the car. It will be of use for the first few months, after which the baby will have grown out of it as well as being too heavy to be carried around easily.

Be sure to buy a bassinet from a reputable retailer, and check:
■ that the framework is well-made, with no sharp or hard edges poking through the lining;
■ that the mattress fits

snugly and is made from combustion modified foam;
■ that it has a sturdy bottom and stable base;
■ that there is a good quality fabric lining, stitched firmly in place or secured by ties, with no loose folds;
■ that it has sturdy, long handles which meet together above the bassinet. Leather handles, attached firmly to the frame, are very durable. Handles on second-hand bassinets can be repaired by strongly stitching a leather piece around the worn place.

**Cradle** This is another option for the newborn baby to sleep in for the first two months or so. Check:
■ that the bars are no more than 2⅜in (60mm) apart so that the baby cannot get her head stuck;
■ that a rocking cradle can be fixed into a rest position;
■ that any paint finish is done with non-toxic paint.

**Port-a-crib** Your baby can use this as a first bed, whether on a stand or on a wheeled transporter. It can also be strapped into the back of a car using a special

anchorage kit, which makes it versatile. Before buying, check:
■ that it has strong handles and·a well-made lining (especially if second-hand);
■ that it is deep enough to prevent the baby rolling out;
■ that it has a rainproof cover to protect the baby.

**Cribs** Babies will be in a crib from a few months old until they are about two. The crib is an expensive piece of furniture and there is a lot of choice between the various different models.

Because the crib is such a focal point in a child's room, and in her life, and because it should last you through several children (and maybe grandchildren), it is worth choosing one that is not only sturdy and practical but that will give you pleasure.

Crib dimensions vary a little, so check the space

available in the room before you shop. Some children thrash around more than others, and would welcome a little extra internal space; so might a baby who is already big for her age and likely to grow at much the same rate.

Cribs are usually wooden but may be metal. They are solid or have bars, or may have barred sides and solid ends. Some models have built-in storage. Most cribs have a "dropside," and many also have adjustable mattress bases. Check the following basic safety points:
■ The spaces between bars must be less than 2⅜in (60mm) according to the U.S. Consumer Product Safety Commission, to prevent the baby from trapping her hands, feet or head in between the bars.
■ Wood should be natural or stained, or laminated, or painted with a non-toxic paint. If you buy a second-hand painted crib and there is no way of checking if the paint has lead in it, it is best to strip off the paint and varnish it or repaint it with lead-free paint. Teething

babies (and even some who aren't teething) love gnawing their cribs, and taking in even small quantities of lead can be very harmful to a child.
■ The crib mattress must fit correctly, with no gap greater than 1½in (40mm) between the mattress and the crib. A larger gap could trap a baby's head.
■ There should be as large a distance as possible between the top of the mattress and the top of the crib, to discourage a toddler from trying to climb out. Many cribs have adjustable bases. Use the highest position only before your baby is mobile.
■ The dropside mechanism must be in working order, and the catch should not trap a child's fingers, nor be able to be undone by a child; the side must always be raised when the baby is in the crib.

*Crib beds* These cribs are designed to convert to a low, small-sized bed which will suit a child until she is five or six years old. The crib is usually larger than a conventional crib for this reason (around 44-60in by 27-31in or 130-150cm by 70-80cm). They may maintain the same dimensions on converting, or in some cases become longer and wider, perhaps to around 75in by 40in (190cm by 100cm).
    Crib beds are perfect for a small bedroom, but there are some disadvantages. If the crib is converted into a bed, where will you put a younger brother or sister? Not everyone wants to own

both a crib and a crib bed, let alone two crib beds. Since you will have to buy a normal-length bed in the end, a crib bed may prove too much of a luxury – though it is possible to buy one for not much more than the price of a good crib.

*Beds* A conventional bed has a mattress on a separate frame with a raised headboard and footboard. The headboard and footboard may be removable for easy moving and storing. Wood and metal are both popular materials, and the range of colors and styles is vast. Your choice of bed should fit in with your decorating scheme but you should make sure the mattress is firm enough to last a growing child for many years.
    Children's bed widths are generally 2ft 6in (76cm), 3ft (90cm) and 3ft 3in (100cm). The narrowest bed width is very good for small rooms (it

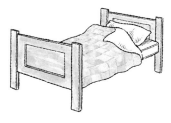

is a relatively common bunk bed size), but is only suitable for a child up to the age of about seven to ten, depending on her size.
    Only let a child sleep in a second-hand bed if you are confident that it has not been shaped physically by somebody else. A crib bed, bunk or bed slept in only by a lightweight child will probably not be distorted, but one passed on from an adult will be.
    The younger and lighter the child, the less she will need a resilient mattress really designed for an older, heavier person. But avoid a too-thin mattress. Foam or sprung mattresses are both good, but foam is better for asthma sufferers as it is non-allergenic.

*Divan beds* These beds consist of a mattress on an upholstered base, which may be sprung deeply, shallowly, or be solid. Beds containing storage drawers or a collapsible bed beneath, such as trundle beds, are generally solid, or shallowly sprung, but the extra storage or the extra bed makes these a good choice for older children's rooms. A divan may need a valance sheet to disguise it. Make sure the room has enough space to enable a storage drawer to be pulled out fully.

*Bunk beds* This two-tier bed incorporates a ladder for climbing up to the top level. Ladders may be removable or part of the fixed structure: you may prefer a removable one if young children are

likely to be playing in the bedroom without supervision.
    The top bunk should be fitted with a safety rail to prevent a child rolling out in her sleep, and the gap between these and any other bars should be no more than 3in (75mm) wide to prevent a head being trapped. The U.S. Consumer Product Safety Commission recommends that very young children not be permitted to sleep in the upper bunk. For older children, use guard rails on both sides if the bunk is not against a wall. Most bunks can be separated into two halves to make single beds, at least until the younger child is old enough.
    Bunk beds are useful in smaller shared bedrooms which would be cluttered with two separate beds, or so that children can have a friend to stay overnight. Sturdiness is important –

many models are self-assembly, and must be fitted together firmly enough to prevent accidental collapse, even with several children bouncing on the bed together; the screws and bolts should also be adequately strong.

■ See page 33 *for high sleepers*

# Space for storage

Never make the mistake of thinking that, because they are small, children don't need much storage. They do, and a variety of it if they are not to spread their possessions all over the home. Chosen wisely, what you buy for your baby in the early years will last her through childhood, and you will only have to extend or supplement it as she grows.

**Bookcase** Strange as it may seem, this is a good first item to buy if you are on a budget since you can store clothes, diapers, toiletries and early baby toys on it at the beginning, and, later on, books, toys and games. A sturdy bookcase will last a child into the teenage years when, if the shelves are broad enough, it will do for stereo, record storage and other gadgetry, as well as books. Put fragile or unsuitable toys and games on the higher shelves, out of a young child's reach. Some bookcases have adjustable shelves, which help adapt their use easily from one age to another.

Fortunately there are plenty of bookcases and shelf units on the market that are very reasonably priced and sturdy. Quite

often they require assembly and come in a "flatpack." A bookcase must be stable. Whether it has a back or not, it might have to be attached to the wall – this is more likely if the floor is uneven, and if there is any danger of a young child using it as a jungle gym. Avoid shelves that are too narrow to take games and large-format children's books, and if possible, find a bookcase with varying heights between the shelves. Never choose a glass-fronted bookcase for a child's room.

An old bookcase could have its surface treated to make it fit in better – either stripped and sanded or bleached for a light finish, or else painted to match other furniture.

**Wall-mounted shelves** Sets of shelves mounted on brackets attached to the wall are an alternative to a free-standing bookcase. Their advantage is that you will be able to adjust the height of the shelves to house different sizes of toys and books. In some cases it is preferable to build in shelves – where there are sloping ceilings, or you want to use the full width of an alcove, or to fit shelves under a window or into a very

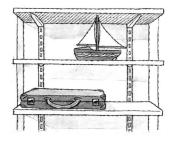

narrow space between window and wall, for example. By building in, you can utilize space to its fullest extent rather than being limited to where a free-standing bookcase will fit.

If you mount a rail beneath a low shelf, this will be useful for hanging up small-sized smocks and shirts on child-sized hangers, while undershirts, nightgowns and other clothes could be kept on the shelf itself. Later on, books, tape cassettes or ornaments could be kept on the bottom shelf, while the hanging rail would continue to be useful for certain clothes.

**Chest of drawers** Provided it is not too high, a chest of drawers can double as a working surface, on which to lay a changing mat, and storage: diapers and all the diaper-changing equipment

can be kept in the top drawer, and clothes in the lower drawers. The top drawer can also be used for clothes once your child is out of diapers and the top of the chest can be where models, favorite toys or ornaments are displayed.

Life will be easier if you decide on a system for

clothes storage, and stick to it. If children know where to find things, they might even put them away correctly. A chest of drawers is also useful for storing toys, puzzles and games, paints and paper. Pine or light-colored chests will fit into most decorating schemes; laminated fiberboard can be painted very easily and successfully.

**Nursery dresser** If there is space, one of these useful storage units, some of which have removable tops,

may form an excellent service station for the first few months of the baby's life. Though it may be possible to find a use in the home for it after that, depending on the design (perhaps for clothes storage or for paints and small toys), they do tend to look like what they are and may be better simply saved for another baby.

**Cart** There are several types of cart, some designed for office use, which have trays or a cupboard and may be more versatile than a nursery dresser in the long run. They have the advantage of being able to be wheeled from bedroom to

bathroom (provided these rooms are on the same level), complete with the diaper-changing equipment. They should never, however, be used to change the baby on, as they are not sufficiently stable. Some kinds of cart could later be used to "file" different kinds of small toys such as cars, farm animals or Lego (though open trays are a little prone to gather dust). Children would also enjoy using such a cart as a pretend shop, library counter, or post office.

*Wardrobe* Babies and young children need little hanging space for their clothes. In fact, apart from dresses, they can do without hanging space for a long time – until you need to hang up older children's shirts and trousers. The tiny, persuasively pretty miniature

children's wardrobes are a charming luxury – they are not essential when children are tiny and will be rapidly outgrown when they are older. However, you could convert the interior of an adult wardrobe to provide plenty of shelf space, with a reduced hanging area at a low level. As children grow, you can progressively raise the level of the hanging area by taking out a shelf.

*Drawers* You can buy storage drawers on their own, to slide under a crib or bed. Some have smoothly rolling casters. Such drawers are handy when space is short, but they may turn out to be surplus to requirements if you later buy bunks or a bed with its own storage drawers.

*Toy box or chest* An open toy box or lidded chest can be used for diapers, bedding, and even clothes at the start, though even the newest of babies may be given a collection of soft toys and first rattles which will need to go somewhere. If the box is lightweight, the baby's toys can be carried from room to room, wherever she is playing. It will be useful for years, but

as children grow older, some of their toys, such as jigsaws and construction kits, will consist of ever smaller components, and toy boxes are not necessarily the best storage for these. Bear in mind that a small toy box will soon overflow. However, a chest with a lid can double as a low table for children (who readily kneel to play) or as a seat.

*Stacking boxes* These sturdy plastic boxes are widely used and cheaply available, in a range of bright colors. Some have casters and can be stored under the crib or some beds. You can devise a

whole color-coded system for your child's toys using these: red for blocks; blue for railway track; green for dolls and so on. Emptied, children can use the boxes as seats and tables.

*Baskets* People who dislike plastic often prefer to keep younger children's toys and books in wicker or rush baskets, such as those designed as picnic hampers, log baskets, or even shopping or waste baskets if they are strong enough. Strong baskets may come into their own later as work baskets for sewing or for collections of soft toys and dolls.

*Hanging storage* Particularly if your child's room is small, you will want to utilize all the available space. Bags can be hung on hooks behind the door, particularly if they are decorative, and of course a child's bathrobe and jacket or coat can be hung here also. Wall-hung small shelf units or hanging cubes can be used to display a child's special collections – of shells, fossils, model cars or foreign dolls.

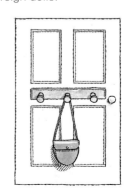

# Furnishing a child's needs

Apart from the crib-to-bed transition, the basic large items of furniture in a child's room can stay fairly constant, adapting in use as need demands. But some items come and go. A night light or a changing mat are essential while they are in use, then more or less irrelevant once a child has outgrown them, though they can be passed on to another child, sold or kept in store for visitors.

While you may be able to do without the bigger optional or transitional items, such as a comfortable chair or a small-scale chair and table, the quality of everybody's daily life goes up considerably once you decide to cater to children's changing requirements. As your baby progresses through toddlerhood to a school-age child you will recognize the need for these specific changing elements of her room.

**Nursery chair** A comfortable chair, preferably without arms, will enable you to feed and cuddle your baby in her room. Later on you will find it useful for sitting in to read a bedtime story. Make sure the chair is of a height that allows you to get up from it easily, even with a baby in your arms.

**Changing mat** This is a comfortable, wipe-clean surface on which to lie your baby while changing her diaper. Make sure it is placed at a practical and safe height, preferably against a wall on one side at least. It could be placed on top of a chest of drawers, for example, near to the shelves where the diapers are stored, with the toiletries and equipment possibly in the top drawer of the chest. Despite the raised sides of the mat, you cannot leave your baby on it unattended if it is on a high surface, and you may prefer to use the mat on the floor as the baby gets older and more active.

**Chairs and tables** Small-scale chairs and tables are not particularly expensive and will be of use until the children are simply too big

to sit on or at them. As long as they can be wiped down, it does not matter whether they are made of plastic or wood. They will be of endless use to children, for drawing, painting, modelling and doing

jigsaws, as well as in games, tea-parties, make-believe and other activities that take place from time to time in a child's room.

Older children will graduate to a desk or work table and an appropriate-sized chair (see below). The low table may then come into use as a bedside table, and a growing child will find endless uses for the low chair in imaginative play.

**Occasional seating** A couple of portable folding chairs may be useful when friends come: they fold away without any trouble and are quite cheap to buy. Teach your child how to open them without trapping her fingers.

A stool is a handy lightweight item for giving a child a few extra inches' reaching height, as well as for serving as a tiny play table or for extra seating, and it will take on all sorts of roles in games. You can buy a library stool on casters which lock into position when stood on. This could be very useful to enable an older child to reach high shelves in her room.

**Sofa** Children will enjoy a sofa in their room if they are lucky enough to have the

space – it can be used for reading, and of course for scrambling all over. The cushions will turn into islands, walls, or even a stage. The sofa need not be new, nor should it be too dilapidated, since it will shed its insides all over the floor, and could be dangerous if, for example, a child catches her foot in a hole in the upholstery. A washable loose cover, or spongeable cushions would be sensible.

**Sofa bed** Though not a cheap solution, this is a boon when friends stay overnight, or to turn the children's room into a temporary spare room. It will have a long and useful life.

If you don't have a sofa or sofa bed, you might consider making some sort of lounging area for your child. This could take the form of a window seat, if you have a suitably positioned window, or a spare divan bed covered with a bright, attractive throw or cover, and scattered with cushions. If there is not space in the room for any of these, try to turn the child's bed into a reclining area in the daytime. Cover the bedding with a cheerful coverlet or piece of fabric and put some cushions around. This makes an ideal cozy place for daytime reading or other tranquil pursuits.

*Floor seating* Children naturally gravitate to the floor, and bean bags make a firm, comfortable seat for reading. As well as serving as a back support, big floor cushions will be used for many games. It is possible to buy a folding tubular frame which turns two large floor cushions into a "proper" floor-level seat.

*Screen* This may be useful in the early days when a new baby is still in her parents' room. It will divide baby clutter from the rest of the room and give the baby her own corner, with a degree of quietness and privacy, shaded from a bedside light.

Later, the same screen or room divider may be useful when two children are sharing a room, to mark a division of territory or to divide an older child's work zone off from the younger child's play area. Some

screens are covered with blackboard paint and can be artistically decorated in chalk by a young child.

Since screens can all too easily be knocked over, you may want to anchor one to the floor in some way.

*Trash bin* A bin with a lid is useful for a nursery: a pedal

bin will save you stooping. A waste basket is essential for older children, who are endlessly cutting out or crumpling up rejected drawings which have gone wrong.

*Bedside table* For children with conventional height beds, a small bedside table is as useful as it would be

for an adult, to hold books being read in bed, tissues, drinks, clock or watch, tape recorder or radio, as well as a stable bedside light. Such a table becomes even more useful if it incorporates a storage shelf or two.

Children in the top tier of

a bunk would appreciate a wall-mounted rounded corner shelf or small storage unit: make sure you install it where a child won't bang her head on it.

*Desks and worktops* The best type of desk for a growing child comes with its own set of drawers down one side – make sure they are actually large enough for the sort of sketchpad or school books that your child uses. Old school desks are sometimes advertised. The kind that have sloping lids may not be much use for anything except drawing, and those with fixed-position attached seats may be very uncomfortable. But the solid kind with a flat lifting lid is both sturdy and excellent. If an old desk is very stained, it can be sanded down and resealed quite easily.

A worktop stretched between two medium-height chests or cupboards is a home-made alternative, or you could even attach a worktop to a wall. A varnished or laminated surface is the most practical. Extra drawer-type storage will probably be needed to go with a worktop: small pedestal units of drawers in metal, wood or laminated particle board are all useful.

A second-hand office desk, not too wide, may be an excellent solution for some older children who enjoy desk-based work. There are also many specialist units on the market for home computers and word processors, often stacking the screen, printer,

and keyboard vertically. It is important that lighting and the position of the keyboard and screen are satisfactory for the child's posture.

*High sleeper* This is a high bed-unit, with the top tier for sleeping, and the bottom usually a worktop, incorporating storage and sometimes a seat as well. It will free the rest of a small room for play, and give an older child the pleasure of elevated sleeping. If children are sharing, two of these may cause fewer fights and be more space-saving than bunk beds and two desks.

Children should not sleep at an elevated height until at least the age of six, so you would have to delay installing this raised bed-unit until then. High sleepers tend to be expensive, too and their use is limited, since a child may well grow out of a high sleeper by her early teens.

# Planning a nursery

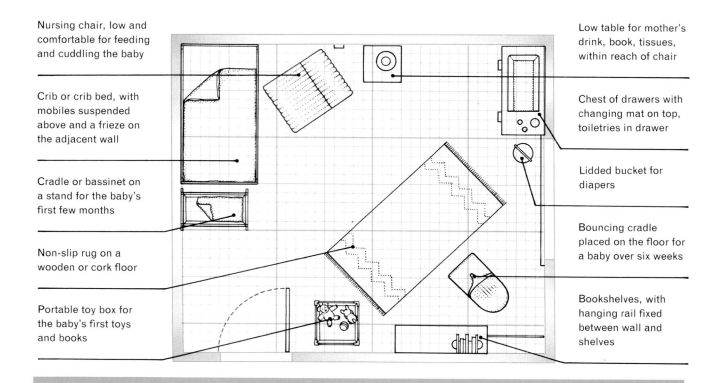

Nursing chair, low and comfortable for feeding and cuddling the baby

Crib or crib bed, with mobiles suspended above and a frieze on the adjacent wall

Cradle or bassinet on a stand for the baby's first few months

Non-slip rug on a wooden or cork floor

Portable toy box for the baby's first toys and books

Low table for mother's drink, book, tissues, within reach of chair

Chest of drawers with changing mat on top, toiletries in drawer

Lidded bucket for diapers

Bouncing cradle placed on the floor for a baby over six weeks

Bookshelves, with hanging rail fixed between wall and shelves

The nursery is where your baby will sleep, frequently be fed, have her diaper changed and be dressed, so you need to plan enough storage to keep all her things – diapers, toiletries, clothes, first toys and books – close at hand. The room needs to be warm and draft-free, but not stuffy. It should not be dusty: a baby's breathing tubes are tiny and easily become irritated. You will want it to be fresh, but cozy and reasonably quiet, with a dim light available for night time. You should consider window coverings which will keep the light out in the early mornings and light evenings as well as for daytime naps.

In the first year of her life your baby will change considerably, from sleeping a good part of the day, feeding every three to four hours, and being largely immobile, unable even to roll over, to a lively little child who can almost certainly crawl at speed, perhaps even stand or walk. She will spend much more of her time on the floor, and she will have moved on from simply looking at things to playing with them. By the end of the year she will be reaching up for interesting-looking objects, opening and investigating cupboards and low drawers, perhaps even trying to climb on furniture. She will play with anything left on the floor, or put it into her mouth. She will probably sleep through most nights, and she will have moved out of her bassinet or cradle into a proper crib. When the time comes, it will make life easier if the room can adapt to cope with these changes smoothly.

You may want the nursery to be as pretty and lacy as possible, and if you can afford it, there is nothing wrong with indulging your fantasies and creating a tiny fairy-tale world – provided you realize that the baby is going to grow out of it very quickly, and will never appreciate her exquisite crib in the same way that you do. For her it is just the place she is put to sleep. Similarly, the young baby will enjoy

simple mobiles, patterns and clearly recognizable pictures near at hand. Not until she is older will theme characters mean anything.

## Down to details

The temperature of the room in the first few weeks should be kept at around 65°-73° Fahrenheit. Thermostatically controlled central heating or safe convector heating with a built-in thermostat are the best methods of keeping the nursery warm, but if neither of these is possible, make sure whatever heat source you use has a correct guard (see page 22).

Some ventilation is a good idea – the ideal is a small, quiet exhaust fan, but leaving the door or window ajar is fine. If the room is too hot, use an electric fan – put well out of the child's reach – or air conditioning.

The floor of a nursery should be covered in some durable and non-slip material. If there are rugs, it is particularly important that they do not

■ See pages 52-53 for *Lighting*

slip or crumple, so fix a non-slip backing material to them. In addition to a night light which could be left on all night to give a baby reassurance, you might like to have the main light fitted with a dimmer switch. This will enable you to see your way when feeding or changing the baby in the night, without startling her with the glare of a full-strength light bulb.

### Beds, storage and furniture

The cradle or bassinet should not be placed right next to the heat source. The same will hold true for the crib. Choose a nursery chair for this room as much for comfort as for its looks.

You will feed and cuddle your baby in here and will need to be able to get up out of it easily while holding her. It should preferably have spongeable upholstery.

As you will often be changing the baby in the nursery, think about a suitable surface on which to lay the changing mat to save you bending. This is a good plan for the first few weeks, while the new mother's back is recovering from the birth. There are in fact some purpose-designed changing carts suitable for small babies (see page 30). But if you do not have one of these, put the mat on top of a chest of drawers or on a solid piece of furniture

such as a wash stand, which is at the right height and which has a cupboard for storage underneath.

All you will need for changing should be stored within reach without you having to turn away. But once your baby becomes very wriggly, be prepared to change her on a changing mat on the floor.

*In this well-planned and versatile nursery, the curtains and blinds, the carpet and the storage can stay when the crib and baby changing unit are outgrown (see page 38, where the same room is shown at a later stage).*

# Planning a toddler's room

A toddler is beginning to understand what life is about, and will have developed a more active awareness of her surroundings, with preferences for colors, patterns, particular storybook characters and so on. She will be walking and climbing and at some time before the age of three will be old enough to graduate out of her crib into a bed. She will be ready to sit down and draw with crayons or play with blocks or other toys for short periods on her own and may listen to music on a simple-to-operate tape recorder by the time she is two or three. Apart from having developed a small library of tapes and books, she will by now need to store some quite large toys and games in her room. Some of her clothes will probably have to be hung up, particularly dresses. All these changes will need to be reflected in the toddler's room.

## Beds and storage
The bed will take up more space than a crib, so you may need to re-arrange other furniture also. You will now want space to store bed linen for the new bed. Storage will need to expand, or at least adapt, to cope with the increase in clothes, toys, drawing materials, and books. Besides providing a hanging rail for clothes, you might put up some low pegs behind the door so your child can hang up her own bathrobe, play apron and jacket.

If you haven't already installed a bookcase or put up shelves, you might do so now, to accommodate books, jigsaws, games, paints and other items as she grows into them. You could perhaps leave one shelf to display more decorative things: prize-possession toys or "finds" such as pretty seashells or lovely colored autumn leaves stuck on cardboard.

Whatever arrangement you have for keeping toys and games, you will increasingly welcome storage that keeps small pieces separate. Crayons, toy cars, toy animals, blocks – such items, and many others, are easier to live with if they can be sorted into their own bag, box or tin with a tight fitting lid, or into a collection of separate stacking boxes or trays. Well-organized storage systems will stand you in good stead later on.

## Furniture and fittings
A small table and seat will be greatly enjoyed at this stage, provided there is enough space in the room. You might also think that now is a good time to buy a blackboard or even to paint part of a wall with blackboard-surface paint, and perhaps to put up a pull-down roll of drawing paper. You could alternatively buy an easel, with a blackboard on one side and a wipe-clean surface on the other.

A bulletin board for the wall will enable your child to display favorite pictures, postcards and paintings. You will find that you get a positive reaction from putting up posters, pictures, photographs and friezes relating to songs, books or other things your child knows and can talk about. Not only will she enjoy these, but they will help to

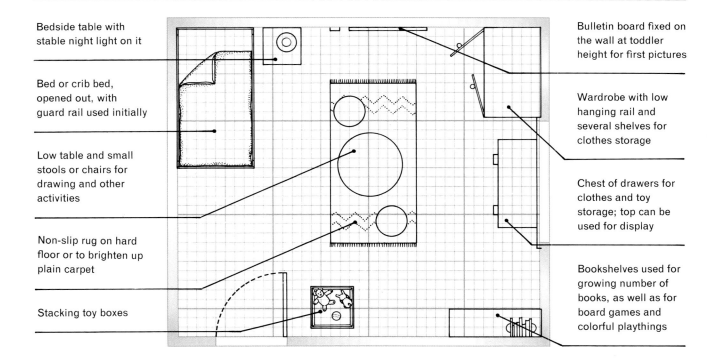

Bedside table with stable night light on it

Bed or crib bed, opened out, with guard rail used initially

Low table and small stools or chairs for drawing and other activities

Non-slip rug on hard floor or to brighten up plain carpet

Stacking toy boxes

Bulletin board fixed on the wall at toddler height for first pictures

Wardrobe with low hanging rail and several shelves for clothes storage

Chest of drawers for clothes and toy storage; top can be used for display

Bookshelves used for growing number of books, as well as for board games and colorful playthings

*Above* A toddler's room ideally features plenty of toy storage, and generous floor space. A low table and seating facilitate creative play.

*Right* Colorful posters and murals not only brighten up a young child's room, they can have an educational value too.

increase her growing vocabulary. Use masking tape or adhesive putty to stick pictures up: they won't tear the wallpaper or remove the paint when you peel them off, and you may want to change them frequently. It is interesting to put up a height chart at this stage, and to start recording your child's growth at six-month intervals: children are fascinated by this visible indication of their progress.

# The pre-school child's room

Between the ages of three and five, most children start playgroup or nursery school; they will be mastering more skills, and – yes – collecting yet more possessions. Diapers will probably be a thing of the past by your child's third birthday, except perhaps at night, and the space liberated from their storage can be usefully allocated to the larger clothes and footwear she will be needing, as well as for more books and playthings.

If your child already seems squashed for space, it might be an idea to take a fresh look at all the bedrooms in the house. You might want to switch things around and give your growing child a larger bedroom, especially if

there is any possibility of her sharing in the future. It might seem a sacrifice at first, but having extra floor space for car or train sets, a good-sized doll's house, or other space-consuming games, and plenty of room to share it with the friends she will be starting to make, will save a lot of congestion in the rest of the house.

If you have decorated the room in a nursery style, you might begin to think about papering it again, with an eye to the future. Or you may prefer to paint over the wallpaper for a year or two before choosing another wallpaper to see your child through the years up to ten or eleven. Plain colored walls of course form a good background to a

changing array of pictures and posters. You might want to change the curtains or blinds too, if they seem too babyish.

## Storage and display space

A child at playgroup or nursery will be bringing home her first pictures or models made from playdough or clay, of which she will usually be very proud. The pictures – or a selection of them –

---

*The wallpaper remains the same as in the nursery (see page 35), but toddler-oriented furniture is introduced. Co-ordinated cushions and wall pouch are added for a new look, and a low shelf unit meets increased toy storage needs.*

Bedside table with night light

Low table and chairs still used for play activities

Divan bed with storage drawers or trundle bed beneath; separate storage drawers could be bought

Stacking toy boxes or crates

Non-slip rug

Bulletin board for pictures and cards

Wardrobe for clothes, with hanging space increasingly in use

Built-in desk or work surface under windowsill, with drawer space beneath

Chair of suitable height for a small child to sit at the desk

Shelves extended with free-standing or home-made bookcase

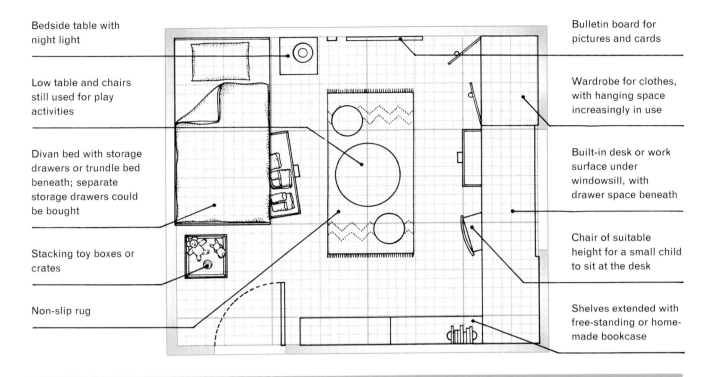

can go up on the bulletin board or be stuck on to the walls with masking tape. The models can sit on a chest of drawers or on shelf space. Again, you may be seeking storage for small items – a cassette player spawns tapes, for example, and you might welcome a specialized, inexpensive storage box or rack of some kind.

Children of this age love dressing up, so another toy box could be devoted to storing the dressing-up clothes collection.

As a child advances towards five years of age, she will increasingly understand about calendars, and enjoy seeing her own appointments, such as birthday parties, entered on a calendar pinned on her board. This may also be the age to introduce a clock if there is not one in the room already.

## Beds and furniture

As your child approaches school age, the small-sized table and chair may need to be replaced by a larger-sized,

though not adult size, desk or table and chair which will be useful for years ahead. You could look for an old infant school desk with a lifting lid – there always seem to be some in circulation – or consider buying a new one. A flat top is in fact more useful than a sloping lid. If you buy a table, don't forget that you will need to provide separate storage for paper, coloring books and sketchpads as well as for all the pens and pencils.

Medium density fiberboard (MDF) is a relatively new material, and more and more children's furniture is being made from it. Cut into interesting shapes and brightly painted, MDF furniture tends to be more lively and less pretty than the traditional pastel-painted wood. But while it provides exciting and vivid types of furniture, such as giraffe-ended bookshelves or a desk on a flamingo pedestal, MDF items may not be too practical in the long run. Before you fall for something appealing, consider how well made it

is and how soon your child will grow out of it. On the other hand, MDF is relatively cheap, and great fun, so an item may be worth it for its sheer decorative and pleasure value.

If you are planning on installing a high sleeper (a platform bed with a built-in desk), you will want to delay this until your child is at least six, and old enough to sleep at a height. But if you are planning on a system of bunk beds, with a separate desk, you might install these now, allowing your child to sleep in the lower bunk until she is able to graduate to the top. But do not introduce bunk beds yet if there is a younger sibling around, as the temptation to climb and play on the top bunk is too great and the consequences too risky. (Each year, thousands of children are taken to hospital after falling off a bunk bed and nearly half of them are playing when they fall.) Choose demountable bunk beds so that they can be used as two singles until the younger child is six.

■ See pages 28-29 *for Choosing a bed*

# The older child's room

The age range from five to ten will see your child through many major aspects of life, from starting school, learning to read and write formally, and making close friends, to becoming aware of baseball and gym, pop music, natural history, developing proper hobbies and perhaps beginning to take an interest in personal appearance. The changes involved in this stage of a child's life will all mean that she is using her room to its full potential.

Toys and games such as jigsaws will become larger, with more, smaller pieces; construction toys and model-making kits more complicated. If your child is fond of reading, she may retreat to her room increasingly, and the demands of homework also need to be handled, preferably within the child's own room. This very busy time means that the room will be pressed into service perhaps more than ever before, especially since your child will no longer feel quite the same psychological need to have her mother or father within reach.

At this stage, you may seriously re-think the decorating scheme or the choice of room if you have not done so already. Your child will have stronger and more informed opinions and tastes, and could even help with the simpler aspects of redecoration, or be involved in designing a mural or stencilling. If your child is particularly keen on some "theme" wallpaper that you feel she will grow out of in a year or two, you could compromise by papering just one wall, and painting the rest of the room. It will then be a simple matter to paint it over, or re-paper it with an alternative, when your child too decides that she has had enough of it.

Now that the messy babyhood and toddler stages are outgrown, you may feel more inclined to install carpet, though you should bear in mind that drinks may still be spilled or food trodden in, and felt tip pens left with their tops off. If you decide to stick with a hard floor, a new rug could be used to give the room a face-lift.

## Furniture and fittings

A reasonable sized desk for drawing, writing and possibly schoolwork will become important, together with specific task lighting. Make sure the chair that goes with the desk gives firm support to your child's back. She might appreciate an additional work surface, so that a construction toy or some weaving set up can be left undisturbed while she gets on with other work at the desk. Or you might consider building in a kitchen-type work surface, combined with open wall units for storing all her paraphernalia.

Children of this age enjoy having friends to stay. If your child doesn't have bunks, an alternative is a low bed that slides under a single bed when not in use. If the visiting child is able to bring a sleeping bag, you can get away without buying a whole new set of bedding. It is probably worthwhile buying a sleeping bag yourself at this stage if you haven't already. Your child will find it exciting to use on visits or holidays. Folding Z beds, camping rolls

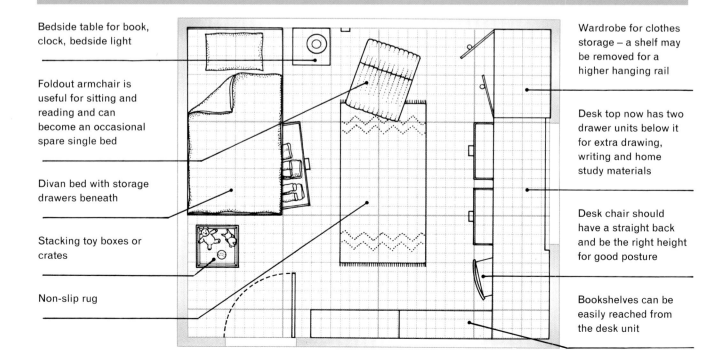

Bedside table for book, clock, bedside light

Foldout armchair is useful for sitting and reading and can become an occasional spare single bed

Divan bed with storage drawers beneath

Stacking toy boxes or crates

Non-slip rug

Wardrobe for clothes storage – a shelf may be removed for a higher hanging rail

Desk top now has two drawer units below it for extra drawing, writing and home study materials

Desk chair should have a straight back and be the right height for good posture

Bookshelves can be easily reached from the desk unit

or futons are other inexpensive second-bed possibilities.

This is the age at which children start to become fanatical about collections, and you may need to be imaginative about devising ways to display them. They may also develop a great taste for stickers, which you may not be too keen on seeing all over the furniture. A compromise is often reached by allowing the child a particular area of the room or the window for such decoration – you may not like it, but it's not your room! Another possibility is to buy a long length of fiberboard and attach that along a wall for a dramatic display of stickers, photographs and other accumulated finds.

*Above* The smart color contrasts of this workspace/sleeping space are extended even to the filing boxes and light fitting, and reinforced by its division into sections. Practical shelving is taken up high to make the most of limited space; the bedside ledges are especially useful and original.

*Left* Having friends to stay is a great thrill at this age, and a trundle bed is a space-saving way of providing for this. The bedside shelf instead of table also saves space in the room.

■ See page 123 *for building a cube unit*

# Sharing – baby and toddler

Most parents would prefer to keep a newborn baby in her own room until she is a few months old, rather than have a very young baby and a toddler sharing. Night-time feeding disruptions and the danger to a tiny baby from an exploring toddler are simply too great to consider this sharing arrangement in any way ideal at the outset. But after a few months have elapsed, or once the baby has settled into some kind of routine, you may feel ready to try it out. You will probably feel happier if there is an intercom between the children's bedroom and yours.

Before you put your two children together when they are both so young, be sure that the older child is ready to accept the younger. A jealous older child can try to harm the baby, or a loving older one may inadvertently hurt her with kindness, by trying to lift the baby out of her crib before she is strong enough to bear the weight.

The best way to deal with the introduction of a new baby will vary from child to child. Make sure you transfer your toddler from her crib well in advance of the baby needing it. If the older child is under two when the new baby comes, she might not be ready for a bed, in which case it would be better to buy a portable crib (which will be useful in any case for journeys and visitors) and use this as a safe, high-sided crib for the baby.

## Sleeping

You will now have to think through the sleeping arrangements for some time to come. If there is plenty of space in the room for a single bed and a crib, or eventually two single beds, you need only decide which side of the room to allocate to each child. If you eventually

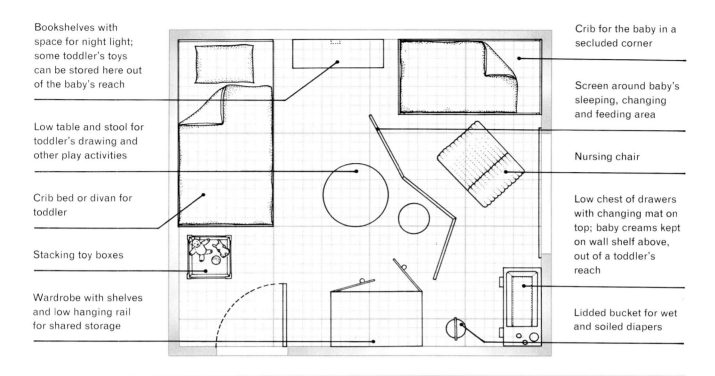

Bookshelves with space for night light; some toddler's toys can be stored here out of the baby's reach

Low table and stool for toddler's drawing and other play activities

Crib bed or divan for toddler

Stacking toy boxes

Wardrobe with shelves and low hanging rail for shared storage

Crib for the baby in a secluded corner

Screen around baby's sleeping, changing and feeding area

Nursing chair

Low chest of drawers with changing mat on top; baby creams kept on wall shelf above, out of a toddler's reach

Lidded bucket for wet and soiled diapers

intend to use bunk beds, you could put the older child in the bottom half now, while the baby is in a crib.

Measure to make sure that bunk beds will fit, height as well as length. Many bunk beds separate into two single beds, but if yours do not, you will have to find a way of preventing the toddler from climbing up to the top tier – possibly by removing the ladder and making sure a chest of drawers is not placed too near. And if they do separate into two halves, have you somewhere to store the other half? You may in fact be able to find a system which you can buy in parts, only adding the top tier when you need it.

*The baby's area tucks neatly into the older child's room; the crib is in a shady corner with nursing chair nearby. The top of the chest has the changing mat on it and the top shelf of the bookcase houses the baby's toiletries, out of a toddler's reach.*

If bunk beds don't suit you, and there will not be space for two full single beds in the room, you could turn to a crib bed. This will last at least until a child is around six years old – though you can now find some models which will expand to full-length. The older child could go into the crib bed immediately, while the baby is in the crib – and by the time the baby is old enough for a bed, your space situation may well have changed, or you may decide to re-allocate a larger bedroom to the children.

**Furniture and storage**
When the baby's crib is moved into an older child's room, you might find a free-standing screen useful. It will act as a divider between them, helpful for when you have to feed or change the baby's diaper at night, or for when the elder child wakes early in the morning. Such a screen might be made of wood, metal or fabric on a wooden frame and it would not be hard to make yourself,

but make sure it is stable. If the toddler's side is fitted with a bulletin board it will be a positive new attraction for the older child who can fix pictures on to it. Behind the screen, keep the baby's things up high so that an inquisitive toddler won't be tempted to explore the diaper-rash cream.

You will probably need to adapt the existing storage in some way. For example, the top shelves of a bookcase can take the baby's diapers, while the middle shelves could be given over to books and fragile or complicated toys belonging to the older child (such as jigsaws or construction kits). The lower shelves could house sturdier toys that the children will share once the baby is crawling, as well as the baby's own toys. You may also need one or two toy boxes, or large baskets, for the toddler's exclusive use. It will help to keep the room tidy if these fit under the bed. But be sure to store well out of reach any of the toddler's toys that could be harmful to the baby.

# Sharing under five

Most children are prepared to enjoy the companionship of sharing, but the older they get the more they need to have ground-rules laid down which ensure that they have enough flexible space between them and that each has some space of her own. Faced with a two-year-old and a four-year-old, this is the stage at which some parents give sharing children the largest bedroom and move into a smaller one themselves. It may save a lot of quarrels in the coming years. Or, if the bedrooms are adjacent, consider whether it would be possible to move the dividing wall, to create spaces of a different size, ensuring that each has enough light. But beware of ending up with two small, dark holes, where you might have kept a handsome room.

If your children are close together in age, with just a year or two between them, you will find that the younger usually goes through a stage of being desperate to "play" with the older child's toys and to join in her activities. For the sake of good relations, make sure the elder has a work and play surface that the younger one cannot easily reach, where she can pursue more complex activities. If the younger child also has her own little table and chair she will not feel that she is missing out on a special place to "work." Conversely, the elder child must respect the younger one's activities: if a two-year-old has spread the dominoes carefully all over the floor, she will rightly be upset if the older child walks all over them.

There will be some days when sharing children argue continually, and you may begin to feel that if they can't learn give and take, you will have to separate them from each other. But it probably isn't worth making careful physical demarcations of where each child can go – they will both forget the demarcations, and there will ultimately be more fights than if they had to work out the division of space for themselves, adjusting from activity to activity. Pre-school children are too young to need real privacy.

You can help to promote a more contented atmosphere, partly through skillful planning and decoration, but also by ensuring that each of the children sometimes has an opportunity to be in the room on their own. If the younger child sometimes plays elsewhere in the house wherever you are, this will allow the elder child to get on peacefully. The younger child should get a chance to play with some squabbled-over toy on her own while her brother or sister is at playgroup, for example, or out with a friend.

## Beds

Prepare for the time when the younger child moves out of her crib. You should by now have calculated whether there will be enough space for two full-sized beds; these may be demountable bunk beds, which could make separate beds now and later fit together, or else two single beds.

Some two-tier bed systems fit with the lower half at right angles to the upper half, putting the bottom bed only

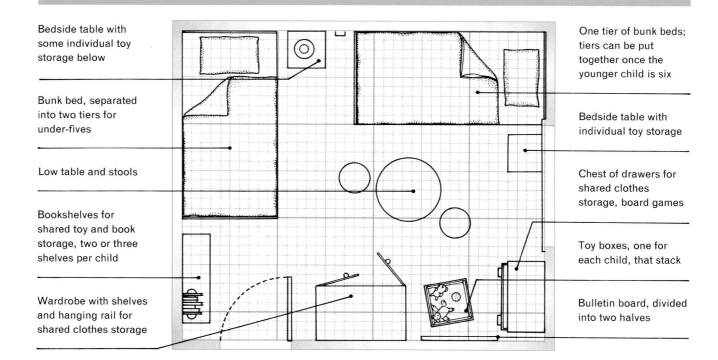

Bedside table with some individual toy storage below

Bunk bed, separated into two tiers for under-fives

Low table and stools

Bookshelves for shared toy and book storage, two or three shelves per child

Wardrobe with shelves and hanging rail for shared clothes storage

One tier of bunk beds; tiers can be put together once the younger child is six

Bedside table with individual toy storage

Chest of drawers for shared clothes storage, board games

Toy boxes, one for each child, that stack

Bulletin board, divided into two halves

partly under the top bed, which may suit you better than conventional bunks and still save some space. If there is not enough space for two single beds, you could use a crib bed to bridge the gap until the elder child is ready for the top tier of a bunk. You might want to look into foldaway beds if space is tight.

## Storage

Your two children will by now definitely need some separate storage. For example, though they may share the construction set, they would probably love a toy box each for their own

special toys, a shelf or two of the bookcase each for their own books or for toys that demand more careful storage, and a bedside table each for night-time drinks, books and story tapes. This bedside "table" could easily be a stool rather than a conventional cupboard with open shelf.

If you have not yet bought a chest of drawers, you will find it very useful now, as your children have more clothes to accommodate. You could allocate, say, two drawers each and keep their clothes separately. Some parents prefer to keep all the socks and

*In this shared room, the older child has the window side and wall-mounted shelves; the younger has a bed rail and a bulletin board – just for now.*

undershirts in one drawer, all the sweaters in another, and so on, which is probably easier when it comes to putting clothes away. But you have to be prepared for some confusion when the children are getting themselves dressed, particularly if they have similar garments and have to work out which T-shirt fits whom.

# Sharing over five

Older children, who are starting to develop different friends and different interests, may feel the need to state their separateness, rather than be lumped together just because they are sharing a room. If so, there are many ways in which to partition a room, provided it is big enough. Those talented at do-it-yourself or carpentry could build and paint quite solid partitions dividing a room in half. Be sure that each half of the room has enough light from the window(s).

Furniture can even be used to make the "partition." Desks, tables or a long work surface could be placed as room dividers down the center, and each child allocated her territory. Free-standing bookcases make another good partition, if they are stable, each one facing its owner down the room. The trouble with using bigger furniture, such as wardrobes, or back-to-back bookcases, to make a partition is that they can fill up and darken the room.

Curtains are a simple and space-saving way of splitting space, and need only be pulled across at night time, as in hospital cubicles. The tracks or rods for holding them can be suspended from the ceiling. Venetian blinds are an elegant, but expensive, way of doing the same thing. It might be enough to have an "understood," invisible, dividing line or to use different floor coverings – say, contrasting rugs, or wooden boards painted differently for each child. Or you could use different stencil borders, or the same one in different colors, to mark out the individual child's zones.

If your children want to decorate each half of the room separately, you could allow one to choose a paint finish and one a paper, provided they combine well. You may be able to persuade them to choose different, less radical ways of personalizing their halves instead – using different posters and pictures, painting the frame of their bulletin board different colors, choosing their own comforter covers or each having a different colored roller

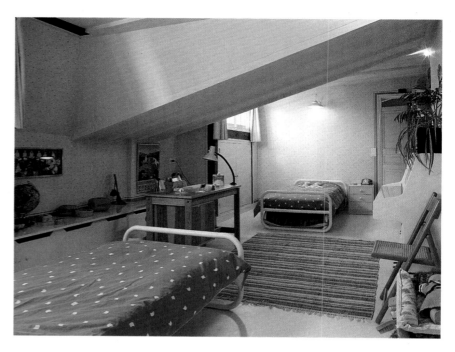

*Above An attic beam forms a natural division for this shared room, giving each child her own space. Identical beds and matching comforter covers impose some uniformity on the room.*

*Below Identical high sleepers placed end-to-end are tempered by personal choices of bedding and other items. The wall-mounted spotlights are a practical solution for high sleepers.*

blind from the same range, for example. If the chosen comforter covers clash badly, you could have two matching bedspreads for daytime.

## Beds

It is more difficult to divide a room which has bunk beds in it, since both children get up and go to bed in a communal zone. But they can each have their own work space and storage. If there are bunk beds, the children may be able to settle between themselves their preference for the top or bottom tier. But if they both want the same, you will have to persuade them to swap on a weekly or monthly basis. If they are both keen on sleeping high, consider platform beds or high sleepers which can be bought ready-made or built into position. They could run the length of one wall and take both children sleeping top to toe, or be separate units, each with their own ladder and desk underneath.

To create a little den for the lower child in bunk beds, use curtaining to turn it into a four-poster (only two sides need be curtained if two are against walls). With an interior light, and one or two wall shelves at the foot end of the bed, this will be a delightful way of giving the occupant privacy; it will also allow an older child on the top bunk to keep a reading light on at night.

Another solution is beds which fold up against the wall, releasing floor space for daily use. You could consider stacking beds, one of which stores beneath another, or a futon which can roll up by day. If you opt for one of these, make sure the mattress is firm enough to be slept on nightly.

## Lighting

By this stage, both children will need their own task lighting, as well as a bedside light which should give enough illumination to read by but without disturbing the other child. Wall lights are a good plan. A small strip light can be plugged into an outlet just above the head of a bed, or to one side if the bed is against the wall. Clamp-on lights can be attached to shelves by a bed – only attach one to a bunk if there is no danger of the light being dangerously near the bedding.

If one child wants to work while the other is sleeping, she will be able to use the angled or other table light provided at her own desk. Similarly, headphones will prove useful to enable one child to listen to music or a story tape without disturbing the other.

## Storage

Storage and display space must be divided equally, though this does not necessarily mean identically. If your daughter wants a wardrobe and her brother a chest of drawers, or if one child prefers a table with a storage cart and the other a desk with built-in drawers, try to go along with their preferences. If the different bits of furniture threaten to look jumbled, you can create some uniformity by color-coding them in each child's favorite color. Harmonious relations are more important than a uniform bedroom.

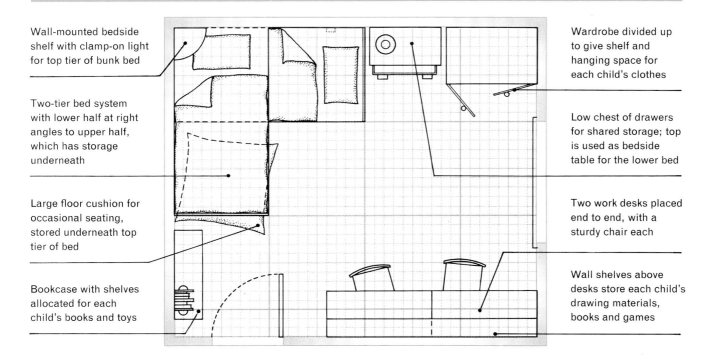

Wall-mounted bedside shelf with clamp-on light for top tier of bunk bed

Two-tier bed system with lower half at right angles to upper half, which has storage underneath

Large floor cushion for occasional seating, stored underneath top tier of bed

Bookcase with shelves allocated for each child's books and toys

Wardrobe divided up to give shelf and hanging space for each child's clothes

Low chest of drawers for shared storage; top is used as bedside table for the lower bed

Two work desks placed end to end, with a sturdy chair each

Wall shelves above desks store each child's drawing materials, books and games

# PRACTICAL MATTERS

If half the skill of room planning for children is anticipating the future, the other half is knowing what is available in furnishings and equipment. You will need to think, not just about color schemes and how to integrate the flooring with the curtains, but also about suitability. Will it last? Is it safe? Can I keep it clean easily? Is it the right choice for the age group? Can I afford it? In short, is it a practical choice? In the following pages, we pose these questions for the essential elements of any child's room: lighting, heating, flooring, window coverings and wall finishes.

# Flooring

Children spend a lot more time on the floor of their rooms than adults do. So it is important to consider the flooring from the point of view of both comfort and durability.

In many ways, the best flooring to choose for a young child's room is a non-slip hard floor that is warm to the touch, perhaps with the addition of a firmly-fixed rug. Hard flooring retains less dust and will also be easier to clean. Blocks and jigsaws are harder to balance and fit together on a carpet's uneven surface and small wheeled toys such as miniature cars won't run as freely. But a carpet may insulate a room better for sound and heat, it is softer for a wobbly baby to fall on, and it can make a room feel reassuringly warm and cozy.

If you are redecorating a room from scratch, think about the flooring right at the start, even if it is not laid immediately. There is no point in deciding after you have painted the walls, for example, that you would like to strip the floorboards.

**Wooden floors** You could strip or sand old floorboards, if they are generally in good condition, then stain, seal or wax, or else paint them. You will need to repair or replace any damaged boards, fill any gaps, and check for splinters. This is an inexpensive choice of flooring which is warm to the touch, practical and attractive. The surface can be sanded again and resealed if areas of the floor start to look scuffed. Floorboards also make a good surface for stencilling. The disadvantages are that it will not offer much sound insulation and it is hard to sit on. Adding a non-slip rug or two will improve both these drawbacks.

A new wooden floor can be laid structurally, in the form of floorboards, or with one of the simple ready-made systems, such as hardwood strip or woodblock flooring, which often come ready-sealed. This is more expensive than renovating an old wooden floor, but the sound insulation may be better, especially if you lay underfloor insulating material (only do this on the ground floor of a house).

**Cork tiles** These tiles are moderately priced, simple to lay, warm, easy to clean, and give adequate sound insulation, provided you lay reasonably thick tiles. Cork tiles should be laid on a smooth floor, such as hardboard. The floor must be sealed properly, with several coats of varnish, to avoid damage through water penetration. Though cork tiles only come in a narrow color range, you can brighten the floor with non-slip rugs.

**Vinyl and linoleum** These flooring materials can be laid as tiles or in sheet form and they come in a wide variety of patterns and colors. They are easy to clean, comfortable underfoot and reasonably priced. They can look somewhat kitcheny unless you use the better qualities which are often surprisingly expensive.

**Rubber and synthetic-rubber stud** This modern-looking flooring is non-slip, tough and comfortable, and comes in a good color range, though it can be costly. The round studs of the relief "pattern" can be uncomfortable

*A modern lightweight sheet vinyl flooring in basic primaries is far from kitcheny in appearance, but is very practical and durable unless deliberately scratched.*

to play on and may not give a flat enough surface for jigsaws etc. Tenacious deposits of dirt can also build up around these raised parts.

**Hardboard and particle board** This inexpensive flooring is both warm-looking and comfortable underfoot. It can be given many decorative treatments such as painting or stencilling. It needs to be extremely well-sealed immediately to avoid damage through water penetration. It is not particularly durable.

**Matting** The usual materials are sisal, coir, rush, seagrass and maize. These types of flooring are inexpensive and warm to the touch. They are most appropriate for older children who no longer kneel to play. Matting makes a pleasant neutral background and some, especially sisal, are available in many beautiful colors. The dyes, however, may eventually fade.

Matting can be bought ready-backed for greater durability and to prevent dirt falling through to the floor. Depending on the matting you choose, the surface may be knobbly, may fray, or may shed fibers. These natural materials do not like becoming too dry: spray them with water occasionally. It is important to fix the edges firmly to the floor, otherwise they may curl and could cause people to trip inadvertently.

**Carpet** Generally, light-duty carpets are recommended for a bedroom, but it may be wise to choose a heavier-duty one for a child's bedroom. A shaggy, long-fibered carpet is an unwise choice for a small child: it will be a dust trap, hard to clean and difficult to play games on.

One disadvantage of carpet is that stains will show, though quick treatment can help (see pages 138-140). Nor is it a particularly hygienic surface: carpets harbor dust and dust mites, to which some children are allergic.

Good-quality carpet can be expensive, particularly if laid with high-quality carpetpad. Heavy-duty flat-weave cord carpet is cheaper and more practical – it is treated to withstand splashes. Some synthetic materials, particularly acrylic and viscose rayon, are less fire-resistant than natural materials, such as wool.

*Carpet tiles* These are squares of sealed-edged carpet, made in a variety of fibers. They are available in many sizes, the most common being 15½in (40cm) and 19½in (50cm) squares. Although somewhat utilitarian in appearance, carpet tiles are a practical choice of flooring. Many are designed to be scrubbed and tiles that become badly stained can be replaced; they can also be switched around to even out the wear. Check that the backing is durable: avoid easily crumbling synthetic rubber.

*Cork tiles are warm in hue and warm to the touch, ideal for a children's room. Buy them as thick as possible and seal them thoroughly.*

## TYPES OF FLOORING

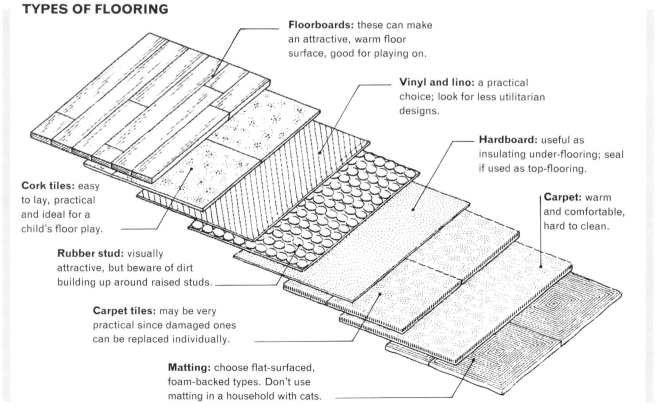

**Floorboards:** these can make an attractive, warm floor surface, good for playing on.

**Vinyl and lino:** a practical choice; look for less utilitarian designs.

**Hardboard:** useful as insulating under-flooring; seal if used as top-flooring.

**Carpet:** warm and comfortable, hard to clean.

**Cork tiles:** easy to lay, practical and ideal for a child's floor play.

**Rubber stud:** visually attractive, but beware of dirt building up around raised studs.

**Carpet tiles:** may be very practical since damaged ones can be replaced individually.

**Matting:** choose flat-surfaced, foam-backed types. Don't use matting in a household with cats.

■ See page 111 *for stencilling a floor*

# Lighting

You don't have to worry about the "atmosphere" created by lighting in children's rooms in quite the same way as you do in more public parts of the house. However, children do have special needs as far as lighting is concerned, and these have to be considered.

■ Babies and young children need a dim light at night for reassurance. This will give you enough illumination for changing and feeding a baby at night, and, later on, will light children's way to the bathroom or down a bunk ladder.

■ Older children require task lights for reading, homework, sewing and other close work.

■ Most children also like a bedside light, for reading in bed, and for switching on when they wake up on dark winter mornings. The on/off switch should be well within a child's reach.

## Planning the lighting

When first planning your child's room, think about the lighting before you decorate. If you have to alter fittings or carry out any rewiring, this should be done at the outset. You might want to wire for wall lights, which is one way of avoiding cords in the room. A center light might seem safe, being high above children's heads, unless or until you install bunk beds and find that the light fitting is easily reached from the top-level bunk.

Consider wiring in a dimmer switch at this stage. It is a very good way of providing a low level of light in a room. The wiring operation is fairly simple to do and will pay for itself by saving money when the bulb brightness is turned down low.

If you cannot change the wiring, wall lights can still be used, plugged into the electric outlets. They will not be unstable in the way that free-standing lights can be. And if a ceiling light is badly positioned, it is a relatively simple job to move it by extending the cord, carrying the cord across the

*Older children need adequate task lighting in their work or study area. Angled reading lamps come in bright colors and fit in well with a primaries decorating theme.*

ceiling and looping it over a screwed-in hook to hang down in a different position.

If there is an old-fashioned fluorescent strip light in the room, you might want to remove it: it will give a harsh and ugly light, and may give your child headaches. However, modern "mini-fluorescents" and bulbs such as tungsten halogen offer a long life, a small size and a bright, good quality light, though they may be expensive to buy in the first instance.

## Night lights

You can buy little "glimmer" night lights which simply plug into an ordinary electric outlet to give a glow in the dark. They are cheap to buy and to run. Some slightly more expensive versions are light-sensitive, coming on automatically in the evening and switching themselves off when it is

light. Some children prefer a stronger light at night, and there are many nursery lights to choose from. An illuminated globe, for example, makes a very successful night light.

Night lights are useful on landings as well as bedrooms. You could put a little dab of fluorescent paint on a light switch to enable an older child to find it easily at night.

## Task lighting

Once your child is old enough to require some form of directional light, and to be sensible about using a lamp, you will probably need a variant on the jointed Luxo lamp. Alternatively, if you find such desk lights a bit too "office-like," you could use a pretty table lamp with a shade, provided it casts a bright enough light, not pools of shadow just where a child is trying to draw.

Another possibility is track lighting. Some tracks have to be hard wired, but others can be plugged into an electric outlet. Make sure that the spotlights can be directed at will: some are too inflexible. Another choice is directional spotlights mounted on a base which is screwed to the wall, and

## SAFETY

△  *Always use fuses that are the correct size for the circuit.*

△  *If you have old outlets without safety shutters, it is best to replace them with shuttered outlets.*

△  *Use coiled cord where possible.*

△  *Keep outlet covers on empty electric outlets, and teach young children about the dangers of touching empty outlets.*

△  *Never leave cord hanging where a child could pull a lamp down, or trip over it.*

△  *Don't leave a lamp without a bulb in it – a child might switch it on, then poke into the empty fitting and get a bad shock.*

△  *If you have old outlets without safety shutters, it is best to rewire with shuttered outlets.*

△  *Be sure to turn off electricity at the electric box before embarking on any electrical job in the house.*

plugged with cord into an electric outlet. Colored cord may go well in a children's room with a "primaries" color scheme.

### Bedside and hanging lights

Young children thoroughly enjoy lampshades with pictures, or ones which are in the shape of some other object – a parachute, a kite or an air balloon complete with basket, for example. And there are plenty to choose from, as well as lamps in the shape of the man in the moon or all manner of animals.

The main consideration with a bedside light is that the base is stable, and the on/off switch easy to reach and to operate. With "clamp-on" lamps, make sure they are securely fixed and do not position them too close to the pillow or the bedding.

## TYPES OF LIGHTING

Small children like a night light. The simplest ones plug into an outlet; others come on automatically in the dark.

Hanging lampshades may have a nursery theme or a simple paper shade could be chosen to go with your decorating scheme.

Task lighting can take the form of a table lamp with a solid base or a clamp-on light directed to suit a child's need.

A bedside light gives subdued lighting. The switch should be within a child's reach.

Table lamps make useful extra lighting for feeding or diaper changing.

An angled reading light is a boon for an older child's work area. It casts a pool of light just where it is needed.

Track lighting can be varied as the use made of the room changes.

# Heating

Children's rooms need heating that is, above all, safe. Your choice of heater should be dictated by whether you can safely leave an unsupervised child in the room with it, no matter how old the child is. For this reason, the best forms of heating are radiator or panel heaters. Any other type of heater will probably need a guard.

*The built-in radiator panels underneath this window seat let the heat out while protecting children from its source. They also enhance the look of the room.*

The level of heating will vary according to whether your child is playing in his room a good deal of the day or is out at school. A baby's room needs to be warm but a child's room need only be comfortable. Upstairs bedrooms generally gain from heat rising from the rest of the house, so do not usually need very powerful heaters.

## Babies and heating

Heating is of utmost importance in a baby's room. Until he is about six to twelve weeks old, a newborn baby is unable to regulate his body temperature so that he remains comfortable whatever the temperature of his environment. Young babies should never be allowed to get cold, but nor should they be over-swaddled in a hot room. Since babies also have such delicate skin, they should not be too close to a direct source of heat, which may burn them.

The ideal is to keep the baby's room warm around the clock for the first four to six weeks. The temperature should be kept at about 65°-73° Fahrenheit. If a new baby has a bath, or is undressed, his temperature will drop temporarily,

so it is wise to turn up the heating in time to get the room warmer before bathing him, if you do this in his bedroom.

Even in summer, the temperature of a bedroom may drop quite sharply in the middle of the night. With a baby's room, you will simply have to use common sense. If the weather is hot, you do not need to turn the heating on and have the baby wrapped in several layers as well. Particularly if the baby is swaddled, so that natural evaporation of heat from the skin cannot take place, the baby can easily become overheated, which is as dangerous as being chilled. A small baby can also get overheated if clothing is not removed before he is put down for a nap indoors – always take off a snowsuit and take the baby out of a babynest before putting him in his crib. For reassurance, feel the baby's skin inside his wrappings (the back of his neck is the best indicator) – it should feel pleasantly warm.

## Central heating

Thermostatically-controlled central heating is obviously the most convenient way of keeping the baby's room – and the whole house – warm. Never have the heating set so high that radiators in a child's room are too hot to touch, or they could burn themselves. It may be possible to box them in with panelling while allowing the heat to circulate in the room.

If your heating is controlled by a set-back thermostat which turns the system off at night, you may need to override the thermostat while your baby is young. If it is cool at night, but other members of the family cannot sleep in warm rooms, turn off the individual radiators at night in all rooms except the baby's. Some central heating systems are equipped with separate thermostats for every radiator: if you are putting in a new system, this may be worth considering.

Always give careful thought to the positioning of radiators if you are installing a central heating system from scratch. Remember that a radiator in the middle of a wall greatly restricts the use of that wall.

## Other heaters

Not everyone lives in a home with central heating. Where another form of heating is used, an adult or much older child's bedroom can go without (though the room should then be used only for sleeping, rather than for playing in, when it is cold), but not a baby's. Some types of heater that are cheap to buy and to run have other disadvantages.

Kerosene heating is not suitable for a child's room. It is potentially dangerous, though the newer types of heater are designed to cut out if knocked over. Kerosene fumes are also unpleasant; and it is a form of heating which can cause dampness in the air from the evaporating water component of the Kerosene. An open gas heater demands ventilation, to clear away the products of combustion.

Open bar electric heaters are potentially dangerous if the element is accessible, not just to touch but also to anything being dropped on it, or fabric brushing against it. Any heater you install in a nursery must be safe for a crawling baby and toddler. Check to see if it bears the seal of a nationally recognized safety testing laboratory, and take great care in its installation and operation. And they should all be covered by a guard which cannot be moved by the child.

The best position for heaters such as radiators is thought to be at the point of greatest heat loss, and this is usually beneath windows. However, heaters which may render the hanging of curtains difficult or dangerous should not be put below windows. Gas heaters should be fitted in consultation with a gas adviser. Always install a heater so a guard can fit round it.

## Insulation

There is no point in having heat in a bedroom disappear to the outside world. If the room has a fireplace, fit a wooden liner, with a few small air holes bored in it, into the chimney opening at the back, or board it over altogether. If you have open floorboards, fill gaps with pieces of wood stained to match.

If you have or install conventional double glazing, be very careful to ensure that it can be opened in case of fire. Plastic film can make for efficient double glazing. Fit weatherstripping around door edges and wooden beading along gaps between the floorboards and wooden baseboard.

The most effective insulation, in order, is draft-proofing, batte insulation, cavity wall insulation and finally double glazing.

Many electric or gas utilities have heating advisers who can visit homes and discuss your heating and insulation needs.

## SAFETY

△ *Fire is the most common cause of children's accidental death in the home. Never leave a child in a room with a guarded or unguarded open fire or inadequately guarded heater.*

△ *The only really safe place to put an electric open bar heater is on the wall, which means buying a wall-mounted one.*

△ *Do not keep portable heaters in a child's room.*

△ *To guard against electric shock, be sure to unplug unused heaters, even if they are turned off, and cover unused outlets with safety caps.*

△ *Check to see that a heater bears the seal of a nationally recognized safety testing laboratory.*

△ *For more information on home safety, contact: The U.S. Product Safety Commission, Washington, D.C. 20207.*

■ See pages 22-23 *for Planning for safety*

# Windows

The choice between curtains and blinds is largely one of personal preference and suitability in a particular room although they do have different merits. Curtains are softer visually and usually insulate a window better. Slatted or roller blinds give a snappy, clean-cut impression, whereas fabric blinds can be ruched and puffed, suitable for a decidedly feminine room.

## Curtains

Curtains can be made of any suitable fabric, though the most practical choice for children is washable, medium-weight cotton. You can make curtains yourself, have them made up by a shop or professional service, or buy them ready-made.

There are many cotton fabrics designed especially for children, some of which come with matching wallpaper and comforter covers. But many other fabrics work well in a child's room, provided they blend in with the general color scheme.

If you wish to keep the light out of a child's room on summer evenings and early mornings, curtains will have to be lined with blackout material (an acrylic-coated fabric, usually pale in color, which prevents light passing through). Alternatively, a blackout blind can be used in combination with the curtains. Obviously, the thicker the curtains, the warmer they will keep the room when pulled. For extra insulation, curtains can have an extra layer of fabric, called interlining, sewn in between the curtain material and the lining.

If there is a radiator beneath the window, curtains should stop at the bottom of the window frame. Floor-length curtains are not practical for small children who will hide behind them and might even pull them down.

## Blinds

Blinds may be made of fabric, but also come in slatted wood or cane, slatted aluminum or plastic, or thick paper. Most blinds roll or pull up during the day, leaving the sides of the window

frame uncovered. This will make for a brighter, balder look to the window in the day. The exceptions are the softer kinds of fabric blind which only pull partly up the window, letting just diffuse light through, and slatted blinds, which can have their slats open or shut while the blind remains in position over the window.

Blinds can be made by a professional service, bought ready-made or, in most cases, home-made. Roller blind kits are quite a cheap and easy option while to make Roman or other styles of fabric blinds you do need a sewing machine and a certain level of skill.

Slatted blinds have to be bought ready-made, or ordered to fit window sizes, and while simple cane or paper ones are fairly cheap, plastic and aluminum versions are expensive.

Plastic, aluminum and cane blinds can be cleaned easily by dusting or wiping with a damp cloth. Roller blinds are usually made in a spongeable fabric, but they will probably need professional cleaning after a couple of years. Roman and ruched blinds are best dry-cleaned.

One potential problem with roller blinds for a child's room is that their mechanism is a great attraction. A tug gives immediate results: the blind flies up and may spin round wildly at the top. Roman or ruched blinds can be lined with blackout fabric, but some types of blind let quite a bit of light through – in particular roller blinds, paper blinds and most slatted kinds – even when shut.

---

*In a room that combines distinctive wall niches with pretty soft furnishings, the combination of unfussy vertical sheers with ruched cotton blinds is a balanced one. The sheers filter bright daytime light and are also a good choice for screening an ugly view. The ruched blinds complement the ceiling level interest of the arched wall niches.*

## Appearance

Curtains soften a room and their appearance can be varied according to the type of heading chosen, from a simple gathering to a more formal pinch pleat. The choice of curtain track or pole will also affect the look. A hidden track is unpretentious in a simple room, but a wooden pole will give a graceful look. Cornices and curtain tie-backs can also be used, with cornices ranging from formal to frilly, and tie-backs varying from a simple ribbon to a tasselled swag.

Straight-edged roller or slatted blinds give a clean-cut, spare look and are eye-catching in bright colors. Paler or neutral-colored blinds can be very tranquil; cane ones have a pleasantly folksy, countrified look. Hi-tech rooms would be well matched by many of the slatted aluminum or plastic blinds, in silver, bronze, black or white. Roman blinds are a good compromise between a fabric and a plain blind: they pull into neat horizontal pleats, but have the softness of curtains. Ruched blinds are pretty but unsuitable for a room stripped for action.

## SAFETY

△  *Fix window catches to prevent upstairs sash or casement windows being opened wide enough for a child to fall out.*

△  *Do not depend on screens to keep children from falling out of windows; avoid placing furniture near windows, to keep children from climbing on to a window seat or sill. To make a window safer, have it glazed with safety glass, cover it with safety film or fit horizontal safety bars, positioned close enough together so that a child's head cannot get stuck between.*

△  *Curtains should not be used in a position where they could be blown by the wind on to any kind of heater or lamp.*

△  *Curtains in an older child's room should not be any longer than just touching the floor, otherwise there is a danger of tripping over them.*

## WINDOW TREATMENTS

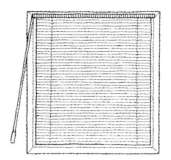

**Venetian or slatted blinds** are available in a wide range of shades from pastels to primaries and in plastic or a more high-tech aluminum or metallic finish.

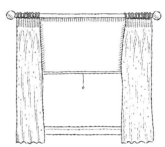

**Curtains on a pole** look elegant and a pinch-pleat heading goes well with the pole and rings. A roller blind can be added to help cut out light.

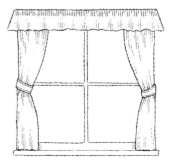

**Tie-backs and a frilled cornice** make for a pretty window treatment. A simple gathered heading can be used when the top is hidden by a cornice.

■ See pages 124-131 *for making curtains and blinds*

# Wall surfaces

Whether you choose paint or paper, or opt for a combination of the two, you must decide whether to go for a specifically child-oriented look or for something more neutral. Do you want to have wall surfaces that make a statement in themselves, or to create a simple background to your child's furniture, playthings and pictures?

Washable paper or scrubbable paint may seem the most practical solution for a young child, but you don't necessarily want a thick vinyl surface that makes his bedroom look like a kitchen. It is true that young children like poking at and rubbing walls with hands that are not always clean or dry, and that few can resist the temptation to peel off paper so that the wall becomes bald and shredded in patches. They may also draw or scribble on their walls, whether they are painted or covered in wallpaper. However, most children past the toddler stage do realize that wall scribbling is out of bounds and making sure that they always have a good supply of paper for their own drawing will make them far less likely to need the walls as an outlet for their creative self-expression.

In choosing between paint and wallpaper, bear in mind the following considerations.

## Wallpaper

*Choice of design* There are many patterns to choose from, including several designed especially for children (see below). The style you choose will depend to a large extent on the age of your child, on the size of the room, and on your taste. Some wallpapers can be co-ordinated with exactly matching fabrics or blinds, or with toning ones. Bear in mind that a wallpaper design may clash with pictures put directly on it, so a bulletin board may be used.

*Durability* A washable or spongeable paper which has a thin, transparent plastic film over the surface, or a paper-backed vinyl, smooth, embossed or "blown," is easy to keep clean. If torn, they will have to be patch-repaired, which can be tricky, or a new length hung.

*Ease of applying* This is easy once you know how, but awkward-shaped rooms are not a good place to learn. Thin printed papers may tear while wet with paste, or heavily embossed ones may stretch. Washables and spongeables may curl at the edges but are often sold ready-pasted. Paper-backed vinyls are easy to hang, but need extra adhesive for joints.

## PAINTS

**Latex** A water-based paint for walls and ceiling but not durable enough for wood. Buy off-the-shelf shades or ask for the mixed-on-the-spot ranges for a wider choice.

**Eggshell** A tougher, washable oil-based paint with a faint sheen; suitable for walls as well as woodwork. Use latex as undercoat on walls, wood primer or undercoat on wood.

**Gloss** For woodwork: oil-based, hardwearing and washable; high gloss or matt finish. Some types are runny, others jelly-like. Use wood primer or undercoat; some newer types need no undercoat.

**Sponged** An easy-to-achieve dappled or speckled surface in one, two or more colors. It has gained popularity recently as a way of introducing unintrusive color and pattern without papering.

## WALLPAPERS

**Nursery-theme papers** These tend to be either bright and cheerful or delicate and whimsical. They often feature theme characters, which may be outgrown quite soon, but are fun in the short term.

**Small prints** Tiny flower sprigs, small geometric or random patterns, or motifs such as birds may suit a child's room very well.

**Stripes or abstract patterns** These are suitable for an older child or a teenager's room.

**Friezes** These range from narrow to deep, featuring nursery themes and other designs.

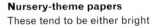

▮ See pages 102-109 *for Painting walls*

*Cost* This varies widely, from cheap printed papers to expensive paper-backed vinyl wallpapers.

Papers intended to be painted over once hung are particularly useful for covering bumps and poor surfaces. They include paper reliefs, vinyl reliefs, blown reliefs, and woodchip. They are fairly easy to hang, although the soft woodchip can tear. If painted with an oil-based paint, they can be cleaned with water, which may be suitable for below a chair rail in some children's rooms.

## Paint

*Choice of design* There is a wide range of colors, but all plain, unless you experiment with sponging or other effects. But you can stencil or paint murals on a painted surface, and it forms a good background for children's pictures. Painted walls can co-ordinate with a wide range of fabrics for curtains and blinds.

*Durability* Oil-based eggshell and good-quality latex paints are spongeable, so marks can be readily wiped off; they are also easy to touch up in isolated areas.

*Ease of applying* Painting is very easy, but it is important to clear the room first and to have cleaning agents, rags, etc. readily at hand.

*Cost* On the whole, paint is a cheaper finish than fixing wallpaper.

Latex is the most common wall paint for interiors. It is water-based, and the better quality latex paints have a thick opacity for which it is well worth paying slightly more: they don't drip on application and have far more covering power, so you need fewer coats. Latex paints that say "silk" or "sheen" on the can may have a slight gleam, which some people like.

You can choose from the ready-mixed colors you see on the shelves of hardware or do-it-yourself shops or, more excitingly, ask to see the color mixing charts. These shades are mixed on the spot by adding tints to a base color, offering a wide range of tones.

*Friezes* range from narrow to deep, and their designs from nursery themes to extremely sophisticated patterns which "finish" a wall. Most are intended to be hung at the top of a wall, but others are deliberately designed to "walk" around the base of the wall, finishing at the baseboard, or to be positioned at chair rail level, as a visual break. Many papers have matching or co-ordinating friezes.

*Above* Wallpaper with an embossed relief pattern is even done in children's designs. This thick wallpaper is a good solution for walls with a poor surface. The strong color choice for the walls is carried through the rest of the room.

*Below* A stencilled frieze makes a cheap and beautiful addition to plain walls. The baseboard forms a convenient ledge for a child's eye-level stencil.

■ See pages 112-115 *for Wallpapering*

# DECORATING

Planning a decorating scheme is when you can bring together
all the practical choices you have made, along with the
inspirational ones, and then – particularly with children's rooms
– add in some ideas for sheer fun. It is the stage at which you
can increasingly see the room come together in your mind's eye,
and when you can consider different fabric or color choices.
Making a room is an exciting challenge. If you thought it was
no more than a lick of paint and the installation of a crib, you
may in fact feel daunted at first, rather than enthusiastic, about
the number of considerations. This chapter should help you to
think clearly through the implications of your choice, and to
anticipate all the pleasure to be had from decorating a room for
your child, whether unborn, a baby or an eight-year-old.

# Where to start

There are many ways to start planning and decorating a child's room, some approaches to avoid, and some apparently wrong ways which, with a little skill, you could turn to good advantage. If you are planning a room for a new baby, for example, at the same time as you are shopping for the baby's layette and furniture, it would probably be sensible not to rush ahead and pick a crib set or comforter cover before you have decided how to decorate the room. You may find that the bouncy bright red and blue clowns look quite wrong with the pink checked wallpaper that you subsequently choose for the walls.

On the other hand, if you have no idea where to start, you could indeed pick a comforter cover that really appeals to you (let's imagine it's the primary clowns), and then work outwards from it, looking for a paint or paper with the same shade of blue in it, a blind that picks up the red, a rug with splashes of the same colors, perhaps with yellow or green as well. You may then settle for plain white or pine cupboards and a cork tile floor or neutral-colored cord carpet, to keep a degree of calmness in the scheme and to set off the bright colors. You could equally have started with the rug, or the wallpaper, but it would have been harder to start with plain white cupboards, since you would have answered no particular color question. You must truly like whatever you start with – whether it is a new fabric or an existing carpet.

Plenty of leading designers work in exactly the same way as this; they collect items that appeal to them – it may be a postcard with interesting colors, a shell with a particular shade of pink or blue or cream, or a scrap of fabric. They use the color or texture or mood of the item as their starting point and look for colors and textiles that go well with it. To stop the scheme from becoming chaotic, they make rules – for example, only three basic colors, or nothing that isn't wood.

### Finding inspiration

There are many lessons to be learned from professional designers and the starting point/assemblage method is one that you can practice at home by collecting items that appeal to you in the same way.

When you see a picture of a room you like in a magazine or catalogue, tear it out and keep it. Try and analyze what it is that you find attractive. If you see furniture you like, note the supplier and find out the price. If it is too expensive, you could visit other shops to see if you can find anything like it.

Collect samples of paints, papers and fabrics that appeal to you. Some manufacturers offer sample cans of paint to try out. Though a furnishing shop will generally give you a scrap of fabric as a sample, you may have to buy a piece large enough to show the pattern repeat if you want to avoid a mistake. A design that looks lovely in a scrap of fabric only an inch wide may be overpowering as full curtains, and a

*The starting point in this dramatic room was the idea of a sweep of fabric in a strong choice of color. The walls and rug have sufficient pattern and the bedspread enough texture to complement, not just contrast with the fabric blind, drapery and cushions.*

delicate pattern that you can see very clearly when you hold a piece of the fabric in your hand may simply fade boringly into the background when you stand on the other side of the room.

Keep these collected items in the future nursery or child's room. If you intend to paint the walls or woodwork, make a few brushstrokes and pin or stick the fabric, wallpaper and other samples up next to the painted color. Do they look well together? Would another color set off one or all of them better? Is a color missing? What floor covering might go with these, and hold them together – could you get away with another pattern, or should it be plain? These and many more questions may occur to you as you survey the room and consider the choices.

Don't forget, as you plan out the color scheme in terms of paint, paper and window covering, that the flooring, the color and style of the furniture and the bedding will all exert an influence on the room as a whole. There will be colors in accessories too: lampshades, rugs, pictures or posters, cushions, a quilt, even cupboard door handles. All these elements, and more, will combine to bring the room alive. If you think only in terms of bringing it to life with paper and paint, you may find your scheme overwhelming when not just those accessories, but also a real child, complete with clothes, toys and books, moves in!

## Color and pattern

There are formal rules, or rather recommendations, about how color is thought to work in decoration, and which colors go well together. While it is sometimes useful to think about color in this rather rigid way, you certainly don't have to be bound by the old conventions. Many of the supposed rules have been successfully broken, as decorators have experimented more, and an increasingly wide range

of paint colors and effects has been developed by manufacturers.

The best approach is simply to use colors that you like and feel happy with, until children are old enough to choose for themselves. There clearly are psychological influences at work in color choices: one person's tranquil room may be deadly and depressing to another. For young children, however, the following pointers may help:

■ Very dark, deep or strong colors are unsuitable, unless used in very small quantities, since they absorb light rather than reflecting it, which can make for a gloomy room.

■ White can be fresh looking and usually forms a good background, but, unless there is plenty of other color present, it may look bleak and offer no visual stimulus to a small child.

■ Blue is generally regarded as a cold color: but this is only true of some shades of pale blue. In many of its tones it is in fact a beautiful and peaceful color.

---

*These two drawings illustrate how the room shown opposite can be changed dramatically by a different use of color, achieving either a soft pastel effect (left) or a bright primary room (right).*

■ A tiny amount of a contrasting color can bring the main color of a room vividly to life. Too much contrast can just make for a clashing color scheme, however.

■ Colors that harmonize in nature will almost always go well together in decoration.

■ Colors change their hue according to the colors they are placed next to. For example, a mid-pink or pale yellow will look paler against white than against black. A blue can seem to alter its shade if you put it next to another blue that has more of a red tint in it.

■ Colors can also affect the apparent size of a room. Warm colors can appear to come towards us, cooler ones to retreat, which is why paler colors are thought to make a room seem larger.

Pattern is important to babies and continues to be so to children. It gives them pleasure and it teaches them about rhythm, color, shape and design. If you are not fond of patterned wallpaper and can't bear patterned carpets, make sure that in pictures, posters, a rug, a bedcover or cushion covers there is material to satisfy the child's need for visual stimulus. But don't overdo it, or you will create a mess – children have good taste too!

# Working with the room

The existing size, shape and features of your child's room will to some extent influence how you decorate it. Two of the most commonly encountered problems are at opposite ends of the spectrum – rooms that are too small, and rooms that are too large.

## Small rooms

In a small room with a high ceiling you have to find ingenious ways of using the height. For an older child you can install a platform bed, and have storage and a work surface down below. Investigate fold-away beds, or a crib bed for a smaller child – the investment might be worth it in terms of the years of extra space gained, even if a full-size bed is eventually needed. By the time she has outgrown the crib bed, she will be old enough to go up high to bed.

Wall space is valuable in a small room and should not be wasted: narrow shelves are better than none at all! Unless you have installed a platform bed, use the highest space to keep bulky and only occasionally used items. An older child can make use of medium-high shelves for books and games, provided there is a set of library steps or a library stool.

Use every inch of space: hang a set of fabric pouches on the back of the wardrobe door or on the end of the bed for shoes, socks or dolls. Have hooks on the back of the bedroom door, and the wardrobe doors, for shoes, clothes and gym bags. A wire grid on the wall, fitted with suspended baskets, would form storage space for pens and paints.

Use space under the bed, if it is high enough, to accommodate storage drawers, or even large games. Install a radiator under a window rather than take up additional wall space, or look for modern, space-saving radiators that can hang vertically or run along a baseboard. A hinged work surface may be a good plan – it can fold away when homework or a game is finished – and folding chairs have obvious advantages in a small room. But always try to leave some open floor space for just sitting and playing.

There are visual tricks to make a small room seem larger and these will work better if you can let in as much light as possible, even fitting a larger window if you can. In any case, avoid heavy curtains which cover too much window during the day; choose light-toned paint or wallpaper colors; avoid large, dominating patterns in strong colors and filled-in patterns that are heavier than those composed of outlines. Remember that painting a room all in one color will make it seem larger, while using the same wallpaper throughout will not.

## Big rooms

The problems with a very large room are quite different, and in some ways less hard to resolve. Make sure the space is insulated as well as possible to minimize the cost of heating.

Stripping the floorboards and varnishing them makes a cheap flooring option. Consider marking the floor out into squares, to be a giant chess or checker board. Part of the floor, perhaps where the sleeping area is, could be carpeted to soak up some of the echoing; two or three secured rugs will have the same effect. For the same reason, curtains are better than blinds and wallhangings can be effective too.

Colors in large rooms can usually afford to be deep and bright, patterns as large or extravagant as you choose. Some wallpaper ranges offer very deep friezes, and these will be useful in bringing down a ceiling height, as will

a chair level rail around the walls or painting the ceiling a color other than white. Lots of pictures or a big-patterned wallpaper will make a large room seem considerably less bare.

A wall of fitted cupboards or bookshelves, or a mixture of the two, will both reduce the size of the room and be enormously useful. A large room has the advantage that it can accommodate a large sofa or sofa bed as well as large-scale toys, such as a play house, a trampoline or a large railway or road layout.

## Attics and lofts
Children love attic rooms. Their only disadvantage can be fitting storage in when sloping ceilings take up so much space, and working out how to cover the windows if they are at an angle. If

*Above An imaginatively shaped alcove in a chimney breast, fitted with display shelves, has created a dramatic focus in this older child's room.*

*Left To maximize head room in an attic, the bed is kept low. Using few colors concentrates attention on the ceiling.*

the attic is the kind that slopes on two sides, consider having the bed or bunk beds free-standing in the middle, to leave wall space for storage. If the walls are very low at the sides of the room, however, the child's bed could be at floor level along one side. Some exciting open shelf units could be fixed to the floor and ceiling, still leave space to walk around. A bulletin board can still be fixed to a sloping ceiling, and you could even defy gravity by fixing slanting shelves to a sloping ceiling, storing books at an apparent angle.

There are various ways to cover sloping windows, but they all work on the principle of attaching the window covering, whether curtain or blind, both top and bottom. This could be done very simply with a curtain by threading curtain wire through both

casing and hem and then attaching the wire to fixings in each corner of the window. Blinds could be fitted on a roller at the top of a sloping window, but have eyelet holes punched through the base (on a small window, just one at each corner would do) to hold the base in position on hooks. Or attaching strong snap fastenings, half to the base of the blind, half on double-sided Velcro to the window frame or wall, might work well. If the sloping window is a long one, it might be a good idea to attach a slim retaining bar horizontally across the middle to tuck the curtain or blind neatly behind.

## Existing features
If you want to retain, but not use, a fireplace you could extend the carpet into the hearth, block the chimney inside and board the fireplace over, painting the board to brighten it up.

If you just have the chimney breast remaining and cannot remove it entirely, consider part-removing it to make an interesting niche in the wall. This could be fitted with shelves or used for display. Such structural work should only be done after checking with an engineer.

# Adapting the furniture

While it can be exciting to plan a new baby's room from scratch, there are all sorts of reasons why it might be neither convenient nor necessary to throw out the furniture from a particular room in favor of a nursery suite. Money is one of the reasons – many families are on a particularly tight budget once a baby arrives. Another might be that the baby or child's room has to double as a spare room, or that the family is planning to move within a year or so. But it is possible to adapt the use, or change the look, of existing furniture and still create a room appropriate for a child.

### Storage

If the room you plan to use for a baby or child already has storage, this may be a plus point even if it has to be adapted. A wall of built-in wardrobes or a free-standing adult wardrobe with a high hanging rail and perhaps a high shelf can be useful to children if more shelves are installed and the hanging rail lowered or removed altogether. Another alternative is to fit a vertical divider into the wardrobe, and have a low hanging rail in one half only. Most small children have very few clothes which specifically need to be stored on hangers. In some cases you may want to replace large cupboard doors with a simple curtain, or to have open shelf storage instead.

Storage such as a chest of drawers will be useful, whatever the style; if it is low enough it could double as a diaper changing surface for a young baby. If it is a tall chest, make sure you use the lower drawers for items that a small child will want to fetch for herself. Even an adult dressing table could be pressed into service: small-sized children's clothes will fit in the drawers for the first few years, and thereafter it could work as a desk unit combined with a stool or low chair.

### Seating and beds

Items of seating such as a sofa or chair will not necessarily be an encumbrance

in a child's room. Even if the children don't use it for sitting when they are young, they will enjoy climbing all over it and turning it into a train or boat in their games! You will welcome somewhere to sit and read them stories, cuddle a child back to sleep, or to sit down to dress a baby. In a children's room doubling as a spare room, a sofa bed would be most useful.

An existing conventional single bed may be fine for a child, provided it is in good enough condition. But an old mattress with lumps and dips could mildly deform a growing spine. Even if you are not buying a new bed, try not to stint on a new, firm mattress. If the bed is high, use a bed guard when a child first graduates into it from a crib.

A bed could be given a new headboard for a child, since this is a fairly simple item to make or to adapt. A wooden one, for example, could be painted or stencilled with a picture, or with the name of the child set into a square with a two-line border or a cloud shape. Alternatively, the headboard could be covered with material to match the curtains or comforter cover; pad it with kapok first.

### Tables and worktops

An adult table or desk will be useful for a child even from the age of two or three. Provided they have a stable

chair with a high enough seat, children like to kneel to draw or do jigsaws, which ensures a good, straight-backed posture position. Later, with a high-seated chair they can sit comfortably at the table or desk.

If you have a solid small kitchen or side table that you no longer require, you could saw the legs down and paint it or strip and perhaps stencil it. It will make an excellent low table for work or play in a child's room and, later on, could be their bedside table to hold books and a drink.

### Decoration

The major problem with left-over adult furniture is that it may not fit in with a child-oriented decorative scheme, or even with other pieces of furniture in the room. But you can strip wooden furniture back to its natural color and then either wax, varnish, bleach, stain or paint it. Two or more different items, given the same treatment, will immediately look as if they were intended to go together, and won't have that rather heavy, dark look that children tend not to like.

Decorating different pieces of furniture with the same stencil pattern will make them look a set, or they could simply be painted the same color in a shiny gloss which will also be easy to clean.

*Left* Painting furniture is effective and quite simple. A plain chest has here been skilfully customized to match a remarkably decorated chair. Dark colors, though unexpected, make a good background.

*Right* Old furniture has been renovated and given a fresh coat of paint in order to unify this budget nursery. The room is made memorable by the bold use of a vivid fabric and co-ordinating stencils.

■ See pages 110-111 *for painting woodwork and stencilling furniture*

# Decorating the nursery

Parents who are in a panic to get the baby's nursery ready for her arrival home from hospital can relax! Research into infant development has shown several things that are very relevant to the decoration of a baby's room. One is that a newborn baby can see no further than 9 inches (22-23 centimeters) and not until three months, generally speaking, can she focus consistently to a distance of 5 feet (1.5 meters).

Experiments have shown that, until they are two months old, babies seem to dislike too much stimulus, or too many jazzy patterns close to their noses at the same time. Most of all they enjoy faces – pictures of faces as well as real ones. A tiny baby might well, therefore, be happiest in calm surroundings, though she will be interested in big, simple pictures and patterns, provided they are close at hand and don't all come at her at the same time.

By three months or so, activity-center type toys or moving musical toys are more relevant to babies than a static nursery poster or frieze high on a wall. Once a baby is ready to be stimulated, she responds to pattern and detail more than to simple shapes and plain colors. And growing babies are most interested in things they have never seen before. They crave variety.

It is not until about four to six months of age that children can focus on detail across a room, even quite a small room. But if they feel they have seen the detail before, it will not hold their attention much. In other words, a baby will get much more out of an interestingly decorated nursery than a very plain one, but only after about four to six months of age.

## The best surroundings

These changing needs can often be catered to quite easily, since the first "nursery" many parents plan is in fact a calm corner of their own room. This will not be elaborately "done up" for a baby, since she is only a temporary resident, sleeping perhaps in a bassinet or a port-a-crib on a stand or on a low sturdy chest or table by the parents' bed.

To shield the infant from light and activity (though most sleep through quite a lot of disturbance), you might like to use a screen. You could make a simple one by stretching fabric across battens, provided the base is broad enough to support the height. The fabric could be re-used for curtains or cushions in the nursery later.

When the baby moves into her own first room, parents can then indulge themselves in the nursery proper, provided they realize that any beautiful dried flower arrangements and dainty picture-rail-level stencilling are for them, celebrating their delight in their new baby, rather than for the baby herself. As far as the child's development is concerned, it is more important to fasten an activity center to the crib bars and buy one or two rag books than to fret about festooned blinds. That said, who does not want to celebrate the arrival of a new baby? And, some time during the first year, to create for her a lovely, happy and stimulating environment is a worthwhile and realizable ambition.

## Choosing the decoration

Once you have measured the room, and thought in terms of what storage and what working surface you will need immediately and for later, you will be free to think of decoration. Good wallpapers can be found in special children's shops, mainstream decorating shops and department stores, and also by mail order. You might choose a paper specifically designed for the nursery, or select a pattern you think will suit a wide range of children's ages.

Abstract wallpapers – perhaps a pale background with splashes, dashes, spots or speckles of color – stripey wallpapers, papers with a cheerful motif such as deckchairs, umbrellas or daisies, or some flowery wallpapers are all candidates for a baby or child's

*This extravagantly furnished and accessorized nursery, in white and soft pastels, is indulgent and over the top but extremely pretty. The appealing view is an important element in the choice of simple white.*

room, despite not being sold in a specifically children's range.

The same applies to curtain or blind material: a bold, pretty or interesting pattern that is not specifically intended for a child can still work very well. But there is also a wide choice of material made for children. If you can color match successfully (don't forget to carry samples when out shopping) you could have an "adult" fabric matched with a child's paper, or a children's fabric used with a paint finish and combined with a nursery frieze or two.

A young baby, of course, won't have the foggiest notion that Paddington Bear or Charlie Brown is meant to be for children and won't understand the associated stories for some years. Babies might enjoy a theme wallpaper, but it will be for the design itself. Later they may grow to love it more because of the books and television programs, but the chances are that it will have become outdated by that stage. A very dominant or rather aggressive paper, involving fantasy figures or fights between machines, is best avoided for very young ones who may be frightened by them. (Even older children may like a pattern in a shop, or during the day, but become frightened when face to face with it inches from their bed at night-time.)

## The white room

If you cannot decide on a color theme, have a baby's bedroom plain white! This idea may at first sound appallingly clinical and cold. But if you are confused by choice, or if you don't like living with pattern in your own rooms and so are unsure how to handle it in a baby or child's room, this may be the approach for you. Even if you like pattern, the white room may appeal as the perfect complement to the clutter that small children's rooms can contain, a calm background for all their brightly colored possessions.

The walls could be simply painted white with a good-quality matte eggshell (a good surface for density of color and easy cleaning), then plenty of color and pattern introduced in myriad ways. To make life really simple, you could choose curtains and a bedcover which match each other. Select a plain flooring that will be a good background to one or two rugs which pick up on a color in the curtains. Various posters or a frieze or two, co-ordinating cushions and lampshade, and furniture perhaps painted all one color, or all natural wood, would finish such a room. There would be plenty of color from the textiles, pictures and accessories, but it would be harmonious, and could never seem like too much because the white background simply throws all the other colors into relief.

■ See pages 34-35 *for Planning a nursery*

# The budget nursery

A nursery scheme planned on a limited budget can be worked in several ways. It may be most effective to spend what money there is on one or two items which will completely lift the style of the room, rather than spread the money thinly all round. For example, you could keep the present floor covering, install your own shelves, and go for painted walls. But you could invest in a new crib (especially if you plan to have more children) and enough good-quality fabric to make co-ordinating curtains, bedcover and cushions.

There is always a big second-hand market in children's equipment, such as cradles, cribs, bunk beds, desks, small tables and chairs, and, provided that you carefully check that items are safe and not dangerously worn, there is no reason not to take full advantage of it. Furniture such as chests of drawers, blanket boxes or chests, open shelving or bookcases, single beds and tables can also be found second-hand.

Painting or stripping, where appropriate, can renovate a hodgepodge of furniture to a good standard. Painting or stencilling several items of second-hand furniture the same color or theme will make them blend well together and look more homogenous in the room. Sewing in a new lining to an old bassinet or sanding down and painting a set of shelves to match a wall color (or contrast smartly to it) can be well worth the effort.

Much will depend on how good you are at making things yourself. Many people find that, though they have never tried before, a baby spurs a nest-building urge and they turn out to be better than they had ever imagined at making soft furnishings or erecting built-in bookshelves.

Always investigate the market first for the most cost-effective way of doing things, however. Some furniture and furnishing items may be hardly or not at all cheaper to make than to buy. Comforter covers are one example, especially when you add the cost of your time. Self-assembly bookcases are often no more expensive than their home-made equivalent, and some may even be cheaper than their equivalent in shelves; the advantage of the shelves may be that you can fill an alcove up to a higher level, however.

## Storage

Storage in a money-saving room need not mean cheap, ready-made units, or indeed any units at all. Strong cardboard boxes will last for years, if they are papered with sturdy, attractive paper. If they are then clear varnished, they will be surprisingly resilient. Vegetables and fruit are often imported in useful wooden boxes (check for splinters) or round or rectangular rush baskets, which are simply thrown away. If you can track these down, they will make excellent storage, either left in their natural state or spray-painted to match the room's decor. Large plastic boxes are not very expensive.

## Decorating on a budget

When it comes to choosing a color scheme for the nursery, bear in mind the traditional basic solution – paint it plain white (see page 69)! White paint is cheaper than any other, and it may be the perfect foil for brightly colored renovated and painted furniture, and to complement the clutter that children's rooms later accumulate.

If not white, then consider another plain paint color. Think in particular about choosing one of the specialty shades offered for a little more money by the main paint manufacturers, and

---

*Right The wallpaper and frieze have a baby theme but the lightweight cane chair and table, and the pine chest, would fit anywhere in the house.*

*Below A spare room can often double as a comfortable nursery. The handsome crib is the one expense here, and the sofa bed converts when needed.*

mixed on the spot. It may seem odd to suggest spending more rather than less money in a budget section, but it can be the kind of investment that pays off. The colors are more exciting than most standard ranges and the paint quality is good. Children love color and are not afraid of dramatic shades, though they will not find very dark shades appealing. Also, you might not need much of the more expensive paint. A stingingly bright green, for example, would be overpowering across every wall. But one or two walls in that color, offset with white, or a simple white paper flecked with other colors which complement the green, will make for a vibrant and cheerful room, and one that will last cheerfully through a good part of childhood.

Another budget solution is to plan now to let the baby do it herself as soon as she is old enough. If you cover a stretch of wall in blackboard paint, you can initially attach to it pictures for the baby, which can later be removed in order to let toddlers experiment. Taking it one step further, you could paper a room in cheap lining paper and paint pictures for the baby on this. Lining paper is a little like blotting paper, so using acrylic or oil-based paints and thick pastel crayons will work best. Later, the room can be re-papered, again in lining paper, but this time for your small son or daughter to add their contribution. Since lining paper is rather like porridge in color, such a solution will only work provided there is some clear color present elsewhere in the child's room, such as the paintwork and curtains.

# Nursery details

The finishing touches that you add to a child's room will reinforce its identity and make it extra special – they help the room to become more your child's own. In the nursery, these details and accessories will be items that you choose on behalf of the baby, while others will be surprises and presents. Later on she will suggest or even help you make some of her own choosing.

## Mobiles and toys

Mobiles are an important source of entertainment and stimulation for a baby, as well as being highly decorative in themselves. They can be bought or home-made, in many different kinds of material, and you can hang them from a wall, ceiling or, in some cases, the crib itself. For a new baby, they need to be hung down low enough for her to see them. Big, simple shapes will be better at first – a newborn baby cannot focus till six weeks of age in any case, and even then very detailed pattern, even thin stripes, will almost certainly be indistinguishable. As she matures, your baby will enjoy mobiles with finer detail and smaller pieces, hung higher.

A young baby does enjoy sound, however, so musical mobiles and bells or chimes will delight her from an early age. Some musical mobiles have a string or knob which an older baby can

*A sturdy home-made mobile matches the wallpaper, and dresses hung on an open rail are decorative in themselves.*

pull or push to make it start. There are also china mobiles which ring out with an attractive chime whenever the pieces touch each other.

You can make your own mobiles in several ways. A simple method is to cut out, bend round and join the ends of a cardboard circle. This can be painted and then have different simple shapes threaded on to it, with the same or different length threads. You may have to experiment a little to keep the cardboard circle properly balanced. Or you could paint a clothes hanger, or cover one with fabric, and hang the mobile shapes from that. If you are not the world's best artist, trace or copy simple shapes from children's books, or look for mobile kits. Even simple geometric shapes, such as circles and triangles, cut out of colored card, acetate or felt are great fun for babies.

A hook screwed into the ceiling is the best way to suspend mobiles. Suspending them on a length of transparent nylon thread long enough

to be within the baby's sightline looks good, but bright colored string or embroidery silk is attractive too. For a young baby, you could hang a mobile from a wall bracket attached to the wall just above the crib, or from a screw-on mobile carrier which can be bought quite inexpensively.

Another decorative and useful idea for a young baby is to stretch elastic or soft, medium-thick rope across the width of the crib or cradle where the baby's upreaching hands can brush it, and securely attach small, interesting items such as bells, a mirror, a soft ball and so on. A ready-made sturdy "crib gym" can alternatively be bought.

Babies are fascinated by seeing themselves. A mirror in a painted or stained frame, set low on the wall of the room, will delight them for hours.

■ See page 137 *for making a hanging pocket bag*

Later, it can be moved higher. Clear, clean mirror glass is important. If you buy one in a light wooden frame, you could paint or stencil your own decoration on it, perhaps adding the baby's name.

Many of the presents given to a new baby can be imaginatively displayed in such a way that they become a feature of the room. You could group teddy bears and soft toys together on a shelf or the top of a chest of drawers. You could hang on the wall or the back of a

shape of an animal or star or some other design, fitting the finished product to the wall or cupboard door with sticky pads.

The crib lends itself to decoration, particularly a second-hand one. You can paint or stain the bars, though this is quite time-consuming. If the crib has solid ends, scenes could be painted or stencilled on the outside of these. You can buy nursery items such as small chairs with a child's name decoratively painted on them.

door any touching little toys or other items which your baby may be given and which are too attractive to hide away – a tiny pair of ballet shoes, for example, or a jointed wooden clown. Such personalized touches will bring color and interest to what may otherwise be a slightly bland or clinical looking nursery.

## Decorative storage and furnishings

A pocketed hanging bag is very useful for keeping the baby's toiletries, tissues or other small items such as socks, mittens or rattles handy. There are some lovely ones on the market, either ready-made or in kit form to sew yourself, in the design of a cat or frog for example. You could also make your own, by fixing a backing to a hanger or length of hanging pole, and then sewing on pockets in whatever sizes and arrangement suits you. You could even dispense with the hanger and cut the backing out in the

A crib quilt is a lifelong treasure which many new babies are given. You may in fact prefer to hang it on the wall rather than use it to cover the crib. There are many different ways to design a home-made quilt, but one is to use a basic background material of one color and divide it into 26 squares, appliquéing a letter of the alphabet on each one. If you divide it to make six rows of five squares, or seven rows of four, the extra squares can be used for other pictures. You could also appliqué a picture relating to each letter, and finish it off by appliquéing the baby's name across the top. Alternatively you could start a quilt for the baby, and add to it as she grows up, with simple appliquéed pictures of items or events

from her own life or family – the exact significance can be explained to her later.

Other personalized items that friends or relations might give the baby, and which will be part of her room from the start, include embroidered samplers or pictures, or specially commissioned plates, bowls or mugs, with a picture of the house where she was born or her name or initials on them. These should all be given pride of place in the baby's room and will contribute to its special identity. Embroidered pictures can be framed and hung on the wall, while china items can be safely displayed on shelves high enough to be out of a child's reach. You can buy special plate stands for displaying plates and bowls.

A frieze is a simple and jolly way to brighten up a nursery in which the walls are plain. There is a wide choice of friezes to buy. They can be purely decorative, with a theme of animals, cars or fairies in attractive colors; these may be found in decorating shops. In toy shops or bookshops you will find friezes relating to nursery rhyme characters, or with an alphabet or number theme. Friezes can easily be replaced as the child grows, to echo her changes in her room.

■ See page 134 *for appliqué*

# Toddlers' rooms/1

Toddlers wobble, stagger, charge and dash about. They are no particular respecters of property, they are interested in exploring everything new, and they detest the feeling that something is being kept from them, that there are shelves and cupboards they cannot explore. They are not particularly good at remaining clean, and their fine motor control – which enables adults to perform precise actions – is in its early stages of development.

While all this is true, it doesn't mean that only a plastic-lined bunker will do for a toddler. Children of this age have to learn to live in the world as it is, not in a permanently child-proofed padded zone. Also, any room you prepare for a toddler in a crib may last until she is at least five, and a much more mature person. Toddlers, in fact, have a considerable understanding about how things should be, they appreciate and enjoy colors, pictures, decoration and ornament, and the more they are trusted, the quicker they will learn to respect property.

## Safety first

It is wise not to tempt fate in a toddler's room. Add fragile things as and when the child is ready for them, not before. If you were to arrange pretty ornaments on a glass-topped table with a floor-sweeping tablecloth, you should expect the toddler to pull it all on the floor and wrap herself up in the cloth. An arrangement of dried flowers in an empty fireplace would be minutely examined and dissected. Toddlers are also fascinated by what you do – pulling out a drawer to choose some clothes, or squeezing out lotion and cream on to cotton balls. But when they try to imitate you, as they inevitably will, it may have disastrous, or at least messy, consequences.

The answer is to put away, out of reach, all that you do not want your child to touch until she is older and wiser, but to allow her access to everything else. She will gradually learn how to deal with it. In decoration terms, this probably means an arrangement comprising some storage that is inaccessible to a toddler. Anything well above their heads, or high up in another room, isn't really noticed at this age.

Even-surfaced, floor-level play space starts to be important now, as the toddler learns to build block towers and trundle cars and trains about. Single large toys or possessions such as a rocking horse, a castle or fort, or a doll's house will not only be much-loved playthings, they will ornament the room. These can all be expensive items, but there are kits available, and it is also possible to make a simple house yourself, papering the inside rooms with offcuts of wallpaper and gradually collecting or making the equally expensive doll's furniture. A fort is even easier to make and needs only to be painted in appropriate colors and outfitted with toy soldiers and horses. A play house or wigwam, big enough for a child plus friend to actually enter, will fit into some children's rooms and will be much used; they can be bought ready-made from thin plastic or more expensive materials, or you could construct your own individual den.

## Wall treatments

There may be a huge temptation for a toddler to draw on the lower reaches of the wall. One way around this is to fit a real or decorative chair rail – a device formerly used about three feet (a meter) from the ground to prevent chairbacks making marks on the wall – and apply paint or paper with a washable surface below this. The chair rail could be molded wood or could be improvised in the form of a narrow strip of specially patterned wallpaper or a stenciled frieze. You could in fact apply blackboard paint or lining paper below this and actually encourage the toddler in her artistic activity. It may be difficult, however, to convey to a toddler that such behavior is permitted in this room but no other: you will probably have to explain this patiently over and over again.

Other ways to create a division between the upper and lower parts of the room are to stick pictures of interest along the lower half of the wall, as a kind of open-plan scrapbook. They can be varnished over for greater durability, and will be good stimulus for increasing your child's vocabulary. As she grows older, words that relate to the pictures can be written on plain paper in clear large letters then cut out and pinned next to the picture to help with letter and word recognition. Some parents make a chair rail-level frieze in this way, rather than sticking pictures all over the lower part of the wall space.

Children of this age enjoy photographs, so you could stick up blown-up versions of your own photographs of different familiar things (ducks, a train, a bus). Alternatively, you can buy photographs sold as prints by galleries, or even use those cut out of magazines. Young children particularly love photographs of themselves and relatives or friends whom they know. Make a montage of some favorite photographs, cutting around a few heads and sticking them over the plain areas of other photographs that you use, then frame the result.

At this age, children start to show independence and get a great kick out of fetching and carrying when they are in the right mood. If you attach some brightly colored pegs low on their wall, or behind the door, they will, at least sometimes, hang up their own bathrobes or jackets.

*Given plenty of storage and display space, a toddler's toys can be relied on to bring cheerful color to a room whose walls are painted in a soft, neutral shade. The curtains and coordinating comforter cover have a white background, which keeps the room light and airy.*

■ See pages 36-37 *for Planning a toddler's room*

# Toddlers' rooms/2

Between two and three years of age, a fantasy life starts becoming very important to children. Older toddlers in particular will love fantasy paint treatments of the walls and ceiling of their room.

## Wall painting

You can do your own mural quite easily (see pages 108-109), using graph paper to plan the design on a small scale, then marking out the wall space in a corresponding number of squares. A Noah's Ark, a jungle, or an under-the-sea or farm scene are just a few of hundreds of possibilities – you could

take your lead from what particularly interests your toddler, or, alternatively, seize the opportunity to expand her horizons and introduce something new.

If even the idea of transferring a drawing from graph paper defeats you, you could make a mural by using children's wooden or plastic templates, holding them on the wall and drawing around them. In this way you could make a small jungle or farmyard or dinosaur scene, or a row of vehicles – templates for all these shapes, and more, can be bought cheaply from toy shops. Adding a simple background of grass or sky, with perhaps a rainbow

**Right** *Personalized children's furniture such as this can be expensively ready-bought or carefully painted or stencilled at home. Painting and stencilling is one way to make different existing items of furniture look more unified. In this room the theme has been inspired by the curtain fabric.*

**Below** *The simple home-made play house will be a delight and a constant source of diversion for several years. The simple but effective mural gives the room a strong color theme while enlivening one whole wall. It would still be appropriate in several years' time.*

or a cloud, will make it into a more complete picture.

A painting deliberately designed so that your toddler can add to it will be fun – you could paint a sea or river, with boats, but leave a child to add the water life under the surface. Or you could paint a blue sky with a few clouds and allow her to add in the airplanes, birds or rockets. Children would also love adding details such as block- or potato-printed or sponged-on apples or other fruit on trees, or a face on an engine. Their contribution may not be brilliant, but children get a lot of pleasure out of this sort of participation. If you don't want the mural permanently embellished, you could achieve a similar effect by simply sticking your child's drawings on the wall with masking tape; this leaves no mark when removed, provided it hasn't been up for too long – for more than a couple of months.

### Encouraging imaginary play

Children of this age have a healthy imagination and will invent games around the minimum of equipment. Their bed or the laundry basket becomes a boat from which they can fish, or sail to South America; a cupboard is a rocket; a row of chairs a train. If you can provide them with props as part of the decoration of their room, you will be amazed at the uses to which these can be put.

A large piece of simple plywood can be shaped into the outline of a bus, a boat or a castle, and then painted. Playbeds – which are normal bed bases and mattresses dropped into structures in the shape of a bus or an airplane – are now on the market. They are luxuries, but ones which will give a great deal of pleasure. Again using plywood, or even lengths of thick cardboard, you can construct your own version, fitting an airplane side with

cut-out windows, or the side of a boat with portholes, to the end or side of a bed. The effect may be only temporary, but will give hours of fun, and children of this age are surprisingly well satisfied with quite naive and primitive decorative effects.

If you need to make a window safe at this stage, by fixing bars or a screen over it, try and incorporate this into the decorative scheme. Painted stair rail bars, cut if necessary to the height of the window and fitted into a rail top and bottom, will not be too intrusive. They should be spaced across the window at 4in (10cm) intervals. You can buy lengths of stair rail from large do-it-yourself outlets. Another alternative is sturdy garden trellis (not the thin, collapsible kind). Avoid it if it has been impregnated with wood treatment, however. Or you could use a strip of metal mesh, painted with one of the slightly iridescent metal paints on the market. The metal can be adorned with a collection of magnet-backed novelty shapes, or with magnetic memo holders to fix up pictures and drawings. Bars can be made into impromptu flag poles.

### Theme characters

Quite often a three- or four-year-old will develop a passion for a favorite character, such as Paddington Bear, Superman, Snoopy or Mickey Mouse. Rather than repapering the entire room in what may be a very dominating look, and perhaps demand new, matching window coverings, see if redecorating just one wall will be enough to satisfy your toddler. The wall nearest the bed is often the best one, so she can lie in bed and make up or repeat favorite stories to do with the characters. The love affair may be outgrown in a year or so (you may tire of it rather more quickly), and it will be a simple matter to repaint or repaper just one wall. If you choose a "theme" fabric, on the other hand, such as for curtains or a comforter cover, this will be more expensive to change.

■ See pages 108-109 *for painting your own murals*

# Toddlers' details

A toddler is obviously more aware than a baby of her own identity, and will enjoy personalizing touches of all kinds. A nameplate on her door, even though she can't read it yet, will help her learn to recognize the look of her name. Nameplates can readily be bought, with standard children's

names printed on to china and other materials. But if your child has an unusual name or you would prefer something more out of the ordinary, you can commission names inexpensively carved in one piece out of softwood, or more expensively made into a jigsaw of separate letters. Having a name especially lettered on china or wood need not cost a fortune. Some newspapers and magazines carry classified advertising from firms

which do mail order children's nameplates.

The miniature furniture that you may acquire for a child's room can always be painted with a child's stencilled name or other simple decoration quite easily yourself if it has a wooden finish. It is certainly much cheaper to do this yourself than to buy one of the very expensive ready-painted items from a special supplier. The painting will be more permanent if you finish it with clear varnish when dry.

Other possibilities are a framed sampler or a simple stencil, unless your child was given these as gifts when she was born. Craft markets and craft shops, as well as special children's shops, are good places to look for this kind of thing.

## Adorning the walls

A bulletin board on the wall enables a toddler to start collecting interesting postcards, sticking up her first pictures and party invitations and for you to pin up reminders of your children's appointments ("doctor 4.30 p.m.

Wednesday"), or the playgroup rotation. The bulletin board can be bought or made in the outline of an animal, engine, airplane, tree or similar shape. You can cut one from solid cork, particle board or wood (to which you can stick soft cork) and cover it with bright felt, perhaps

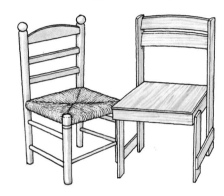

sewing on extra features such as eyes or a tail. A large bulletin board from a shop will look more exciting if its plain frame is painted.

A measuring chart fixed to the wall will begin to interest children around

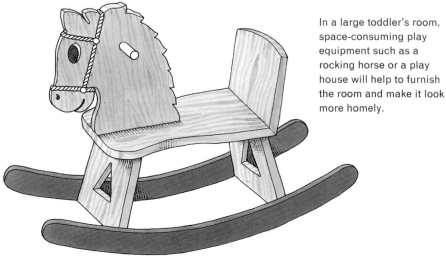

In a large toddler's room, space-consuming play equipment such as a rocking horse or a play house will help to furnish the room and make it look more homely.

the age of three, though of course you can start it before then as a height record. Again, these can either be bought or, if you prefer, home made, by drawing a tall, jolly figure to a height of five or more feet (one and half meters), and carefully measuring off inch gradations from a steel rule at right angles to the floor; make sure the floor is level first, by using a plumbline or carpenter's level. You could do this straight on to the wall, or a door, but it might well be safer drawn on a length of thick paper mounted on a board, in case you wanted to decorate over the wall surface.

Clothes hooks or pegs will come into

*A charming indoor "window box" of cut-out flowers might be fun to make with your toddler one day. The theme could alternatively be a row of birds or soldiers.*

their own at this stage for having a jacket or bathrobe hung on them. They are jolly in bright colors, and there are many made from wood or plastic specifically for children, incorporating the shape of an animal or fruit. You can buy pegs individually, or in a row on a single backboard. Fix them low enough for a child to reach.

Pegs may have another use too – dressing up is a favorite pastime of this age group. While you may have a dressing up box or some "let's pretend" clothes in a drawer, it may also be fun to have a selection of hats – a fireman's helmet, hard hat, Indian headdress, policeman's cap, frilly bonnet and so on – which can be hung on low pegs as much for their decorative value as for their practical use. Cheap hats like these can be bought in many toy shops or department stores.

Masks can also be something exciting to hang up, or stick up on the wall, providing they are not too frightening. Necklaces and ribbons can look good hung up in this way, perhaps on a piece of painted board

with cup hooks screwed in. Children also seem to start acquiring brooches and badges at an early age: these could be kept pinned to a felt-covered board when they are not adorning the children's clothes.

## Soft furnishings

Cushions are great fun for children and make as suitable a finishing touch for a child's room as for the sitting room sofa. Bought cushions can be made more interesting by cutting out and sewing on appliqué shapes; neat blanket stitch is an alternative to machine sewing, and you might make a feature of the blanket stitch by using a contrasting color thread. You could appliqué a cushion for each letter of the child's name, so that the cushions spell it out when arranged in a row. But if your child's name is too long, try numbers from one to five, or just cheerful shapes. There are knitting kits available which result in a real knitted scene, with knobbly sheep and puffy smoke from an engine. And needlepoint, for example, can be excitingly adapted for children.

Rugs are another finishing touch which can be bought with a child in mind. Wool or synthetic-fiber rugs with favorite children's motifs can be found in the shops. Some are actually cut out in the shape of a particular animal or character. Since toddlers spend so much time on the floor, they will become very friendly with such a rug.

■ See pages 132-134 *for Making cushions*

# Shared solutions

Robustness, storage and play space are obviously twice as important where two or more children will share a room. But some children are temperamentally more suited to a sharing situation than others. Those that get along together easily may manage with no special provision apart from some separate storage and their own bed; everything else will just be "ours." Younger ones who have known no alternative are generally more likely to take this for granted. But certain sharing children need much more careful handling. The age of the children concerned is the other crucial factor to take into consideration when decorating a shared room.

### Three and five years
Rather than have the younger child overpowered with a violent wallpaper or the elder still living with a nursery theme, it might be better if a compromise were chosen for siblings of this age. Both children will prefer a choice that they have been involved with, whether it is paint or wallpaper. You could choose a wallpaper they both like, or let each child have his or her favourite color as paint on the walls – if they happen to have preferred colors that will go well together.

You will have to treat a dual color choice carefully, but it can help to give a room a strong identity. Suppose one child loves blue and the other green. You need to find two shades of these colors that are harmonious and you could then paint opposite walls, leaving the other two walls white. Or you might find a good wallpaper that contains both colors and go for that. Alternatively, paint one wall in contrasting stripes of the two colors, or with big circles of blue and green on a plain background.

You could continue the process in a co-ordinated way throughout the room, with drawer fronts and shelves being given the alternating treatment and each child storing clothes and books in the appropriately-colored spaces.

Storage boxes, lamps and other accessories can also be bought in the individually chosen colors.

If such bold schemes are not your idea of good decoration, a more tranquil effect could be achieved with a stencil pattern in the chosen colors on a plain background, or, more adventurously, by lightly spattering a plain wall with the two colors in paint form. Clear-lacquer the wall when dried for a professional finish.

### Eight and ten years
The main decision for older children close in age is whether to treat them equally by giving them identical things (same comforter cover, same bedside rug, same lamp) or to treat them fairly by letting each one choose what he or she wants, ensuring that roughly the same amount of money, time or trouble is spent on each. The disadvantage of an identically twinned room is that it might look a bit like a hotel room, and be claustrophobic to each child's developing personality. The disadvantage of having nothing the same is that it could appear chaotic. You might quite reasonably decide that the positive effects of letting each child choose for herself outweigh any incoherence of style: what is the point of a beautifully

*Right* In this uncluttered, vivid room shared by older children, there is similarity without twinning, some separation and some sharing. One child sleeps high, the other low, and each has a storage box with his or her initial letter boldly painted on. The children each have their own work surface, but share the clothes storage.

*Below* The identical solution has been unashamedly carried through with complete confidence in this room shared by pre-school children. This can have a great impact but may prove constricting in the long run as children seek to assert their own personalities.

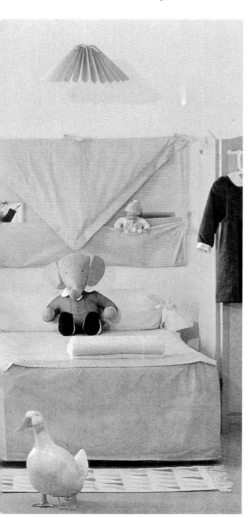

matching room if there are two fed-up children in it?

A middle road is to choose some identical, or partnered, elements around which the children can go off in their different directions. For example, you might choose bunk beds with a red tubular steel frame and put up two sets of shelves. The children together could pick out a wallpaper and blind on which they agreed. (One way to get them to agree is to tell them that you will choose if they can't.) They could each be allowed their choice of comforter cover, rug, desk, chair, lamp and pictures, the only proviso being that what they choose does not positively clash with the bunk-bed red, the wallpaper and blind, or with each other. There is enough choice around to ensure that making or finding something acceptable within such limits is not impossible.

Older children need their own work space, so it is important to provide each child with a good-sized desk or table plus a chair, a light and some desk-top storage. But since they are older and taller, you could make space for this by moving shelving higher up the wall and providing movable steps, or by constructing or buying raised

beds. Hanging space for clothes may become important too. If they use the same rail or wardrobe, you could give each their own hangers for differentiation – there are good-colored, strong plastic ones on the market, or you could paint wooden ones in two separate colors.

It might be an idea to allot each child his or her own space for posters and pictures, so that, for example, the nature pictures aren't driven out by the pictures of pop stars, nor fights forever developing over football players versus tennis players. You could "frame" the display areas with a colored border, or attach separate bulletin boards.

The usefulness of room dividers depends on the psychological needs of the children. Some become quite anxious about needing their own private space, others continue to be happy to live open-plan. If a girl and boy are sharing, and will have to continue to do so, this would be a good age to introduce a room divider for the sake of privacy. Try and make a division so that both halves of the room receive natural light, and as far as possible aim to create a form of divider that appears to be an integrated part of the decorative scheme of the room.

■ See pages 42-47 *for planning shared rooms*

# A five-year old's room

The age of five or six is one of the turning points for children. They start school if they have not already done so, and before your eyes they seem to gain in maturity quite quickly. Their room will increasingly become a private retreat to take their new schoolfriends to, as well as the place where they can put new-found skills into action – model-making, reading, drawing, writing – and all the other hobbies of childhood.

So when it comes to designing the bedroom for your five-year-old, do it with your particular child in mind. Ask yourself all the time how she will use the room and whether your choice is really best for this individual. And ask her opinion too. Children have to learn to make choices in life, and practice is very useful for them. They will be delighted to be treated like an adult and will love their room much more if they feel they have helped to make it.

## Controlling the choice
Some parents are wary of involving their children because they are alarmed at the thought of what they might choose. But there are ways around this risk, of letting children feel involved without necessarily allowing them complete control. For example, include samples of fabric or wallpaper that they like in the shop or catalog in the batch that you will try out at home. It will be good for their self-esteem that you have taken them seriously – and they may not be quite so keen on their own choice after seeing it in context for a few days. Conversely, they may become even more convinced of the suitability of their choice, and you may have discovered a way to incorporate it into the decorating scheme. It is, after all, their room, not yours.

Alternatively, ask your children to contribute ideas that you can work into a scheme. For example, ask for their three favorite colors, in order. Or try approaches which offer a degree of control, such as "If you could have a

picture stencilled on the wall, what would it be?" or "Which of these do you think would look nicest on your cupboard?" If you want to gain an idea of their likes and dislikes without their trying to please you, suggest that you play a game in the shop, finding out which the best curtains are, without saying that you are thinking of making them new curtains. Children are keen to please adults, surprised though many adults might be to hear it, and will often pick what they think *you* will like, in an attempt to gain your approval.

That said, the idea of a co-ordinating scheme rather baffles younger children, who are likely to look at the comforter cover quite separately from the curtains and both in isolation from the floor covering. It is hard for a young child to see that the bright green comforter cover decorated with lurid yellow bananas would probably clash horribly with the already-chosen red and white gingham curtains – the two items are simply both very appealing in a young child's eyes.

As before, if a child takes a passionate fancy to a wallpaper that you are convinced will be a passing fad, you don't have to humor her completely. Offer to paper just one wall, or just the cupboard door fronts, which will be easier to obliterate later when the fad has faded. Soft furnishings are unfortunately rather more permanent and cost more. They can be turned into cushion covers or patchwork, but the passing fancy will have cost you a lot of money, so it may be advisable not to indulge your child's choice of fabric if you feel it is too extreme to live with.

## Adapting ideas
If your child knows quite a few other children, ask if there is anything she particularly likes or dislikes about her friends' rooms. Some of the answers will be irrelevant – she may like a room just because it has a toy that she loves playing with when she visits. But you may glean clues about what she really

*This pleasant and traditional room could remain basically unchanged for several years: the patterned wallpaper, zigzag cornice, patchwork quilt and painted furniture will still please an older child, while toys, chair and lampshade will change.*

thinks is important. Don't try and simply copy ideas wholesale though: they won't look as good as in the room they were planned for and it will give your child a bad model of creativity.

There's nothing wrong in picking up and adapting an idea, however. Perhaps one of your child's friends has a mock "four-poster" made by erecting a framework canopy and drapes around her bed. You could do the same, but with a different fabric and trimming, and thus please everybody – children like feeling they have something in common with a friend.

## A rational approach
Encourage children to think about how they use furniture and accessories when discussing possible purchases and plans. Will a lamp with a top switch or a switch on a cord be most useful? Would they actually like a bunk bed or will it be a bore to have to go up and down a ladder all the time? Will this bookcase fit into that space? It will help them to think about their environment logically, as well as about measurements and use of space.

At the same time, you should not expect too much of a child of this age. If you can see that she loves construction kits, and has always enjoyed making collages out of old cereal boxes and glue, then it's up to you to see that a work surface or a good-sized table will be particularly important for her. No child of this age is likely to say, "Oh and don't forget, Mommy, I'll need a lot of work surface because in two or three years' time I'll be building really complicated construction kits and will have set up a weaving loom."

■ See pages 38-41 *for planning rooms for the pre-school and the older child*

# Five years and beyond

Space and sturdiness are both great assets in a room for a child of this age. Five- and six-year-olds are continually adding new abilities and possessions to their lives, but they haven't necessarily given up on old favorites. They will often turn back to pre-school toys, finding new ways to play with them, or just enjoying the reassurance of finding that they haven't changed. Meanwhile, they can climb like monkeys, and love turning their room into a mini gym, jumping and wrestling and bouncing – and rarely remembering to take their shoes off unless they are reminded. Wallpaper will inevitably get scuffed and the furniture may be used as a springboard rather too frequently.

## Decorating to last

It is important that, from the age of five, a child's room is decorated in a robust and practical way. You might think about choosing a flooring which can be extended up the walls, such as sturdy rubber stud, which comes in pastel or bright colors. The baseboard would have to be removed, or the rubber stud started immediately above the skirting.

Low-level wood panelling is another possibility; painted, it would give a "chalet" feel to a room, and looks particularly attractive when painted in a light, soft color such as pink, grey-blue, milky green or white. Cork tiles or sheeting on the wall, or walls, would be warm and cozy, and makes an

excellent surface on to which to pin children's pictures. Even and straight walls are important for cork, however, as tile irregularities look ugly. Another alternative would be to stretch felt, hessian or another material over the cork with a non-staining glue or with small fixing pins.

An expensive but effective treatment for the lower levels of walls is to stick posters and pictures behind a layer of clear plexiglass. If you prefer to stick to wallpaper, some types can be protected by clear polyurethane varnish. Either check with the manufacturers, or test a section first, however, as such treatment may cause a yellowing of the surface. On application varnish will of course make the paper wet, and vulnerable to tearing until it dries.

Eggshell is a not-too-glossy, oil-based paint which is washable and could be used for the walls. If bought from a manufacturer's mix-to-specification range, eggshell paint is available in an attractive and unusual range of colors.

Simply removing the present baseboard and laying a deeper one is an alternative form of protection for the lower reaches of the walls. It could be left plain or be stencilled – provided a baseboard is actually clean, there is something very charming about a worn stencil pattern, and it is perfectly possible to be frankly nostalgic about the scuffs and dents of childhood when surveying a chipped wall.

**Left** *The graphic wallpaper makes a calm but colorful background against which more storage and other furniture can be added as necessary: the basic elements of a sub-teens bedroom are already in place.*

**Right** *The high-technology influence is present in the choice of furniture and storage, but the primaries color scheme keeps the room cheerful and child-oriented.*

## Furnishing for growing needs

It is important to think about your child's future as well as present size and activities when decorating and furnishing her room.

Medium-density fiberboard (MDF) children's furniture, beautifully painted, is springing up everywhere. This is an extremely good material to work with: strong, not too expensive and easy to cut and shape. As a novelty and charming decoration, it is a splendid idea – a little bookcase between two sides shaped and painted like elephants, giraffes or giant parrots is tempting and will certainly grace a room. There is nothing wrong in falling for this kind of furniture, which makes excellent little tables and chairs, cupboards and boxes, and bigger items too. But do not make the mistake of thinking that such a bookcase, for example, will hold every book your child will ever have. Some such bookcases, indeed, seem designed to hold only Beatrix Potter-sized books.

It is important to bear in mind the height and width, not just of paperbacks but also of children's encyclopedias, reference books, sketch-pads and school files when choosing a bookcase to last for the next few years. By all means have the decorative bookcase, but make sure that you also have enough sturdy shelving for plenty of books and games as well. If there isn't room to have both, be content with what you can get most books and games on. You could always use jolly bookends, which are sold in pairs, to sit on top of a chest of drawers or other piece of furniture to liven up the room.

# Details for five-year-olds

From about the age of five, children seem to feel the need to mark out their own territory: the ubiquitous stickers appear all over their beds and they start using new-found writing skills for notes stuck on the doors of their room, often threatening dire consequences should anyone dare to enter. Rather than fight the tendency, it is probably better simply to seek to direct it.

The trouble with younger children is that they often put their stickers all crammed together in a corner, usually in a lop-sided fashion. Try to help them to think more about display. A collection of stickers jauntily displayed over a window or a bedstead can look very good – to their eyes at least – and can easily be added to by friends and relations or as souvenirs of a holiday or special outing. If you really can't bear for windows, walls or furniture to receive the sticker treatment, fix up a big board covered with plastic laminate for the purpose.

This is the age at which novelty items and decorative touches will be most appreciated. Accessories such as pajama or nightgown cases can be amusing and may stay with a child until their teenage years or beyond. It is also possible to track down fun pillows in the form of cartoon or other creatures which have arms, legs, hats and clothes. Their disadvantage is that generally they have to be sponge-washed and rinsed because of their filling and the variety of different materials that are used in their

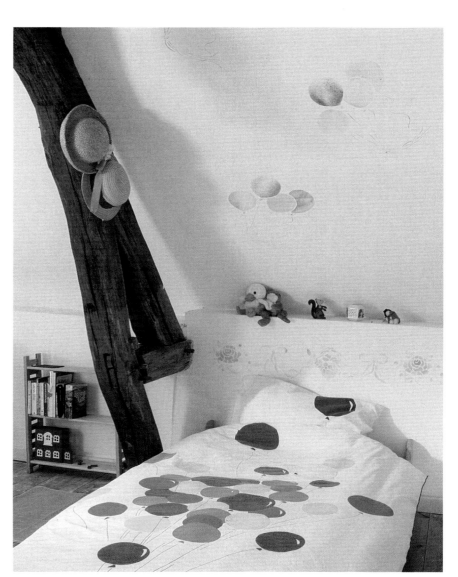

construction. But they will be great favorites. You could make simpler versions yourself by adapting pillowcases to take arms and legs attached with sewn-on thin Velcro strips, and sewing bodies on the case made out of machine-washable pieces of cotton fabric.

A decorative cornice provides an attractive finishing touch. You can make one from a lightweight box which can be fitted to the top of the window, perhaps cut out in a clever shape such

*Straw hats are a simple way of embellishing a dramatic old roof beam.*

as a battlement or a row of scallops, and covered with material matching or contrasting with the curtains or blind, or even with a little collaged scene. For more details on window treatments, including cornices, see pages 124-131.

The waste basket might not sound a promising zone for a finishing touch, but in fact a plain metal one could be covered with pictures, or painted, to make a utility item part of the furniture. It might also encourage your child to remember that it is there when she is cutting out or engaged in another mess-making activity.

Some children have a road or train layout fixed permanently on to a large sheet of solid particle board or hardboard. This saves laying it out every time it is played with, and saves floor space too – the board can be stood against the wall or stored under a bed. If it is to stand against a wall, it can add to the decorative aspects of the rooms by being embellished as a portable mural. You could paint it up as a real scene, whether in town or country, and stick model houses, animals and so on to it, with papier-mâché or model-makers' hills and trees glued on.

### Playing and learning
For budding artists, you can buy a giant paper holder, designed to take drawing paper on a big roll, which can be attached to the wall and the paper pulled down as needed. An easel is another good idea if you don't already have one; make sure there is room to put the paints on a shelf or ledge at the base of the painting board. You can also attach painting paper to the easel with easily-removable masking tape.

Children will be learning to tell the time now, and though a clearly marked-out face is better for the actual learning process, an attractive clock with a painted or decorated face will furnish the room well, and will probably be a much-loved feature. Avoid cuckoo clocks, however, if you don't want to be driven mad (and your child woken up) all night long. Time can be the basis of other ideas for a five-year-old: calendars, birthday charts and, at Christmas, Advent calendars. A calendar with a month to a page and with large enough squares for each day to take childish handwriting is the most useful.

As this is the age at which the first desk or work table is often acquired, some form of table-top storage will both be useful and will make your child feel very important. A desk organizer will hold pens and pencils, paper clips, elastic bands, pencil sharpeners and erasers, and a letter rack can hold postcards and stationery.

### Small storage ideas
Since the pleasure of owning, arranging and displaying is strong, you could turn it to good use by perhaps investing in one or two plastic tool boxes divided into compartments. These can be used to sort and store different sized and colored components of construction sets, like the smaller-sized Lego, or play figures with accessories which children of this age are moving on to. Tool boxes will always be useful, and a five-year-old loves their smart, organized look. One could be used as a first sewing box, too, for sorting buttons, different colored embroidery cottons or weaving wools, and ribbons and trimmings for those starting craftwork at an early stage in their life.

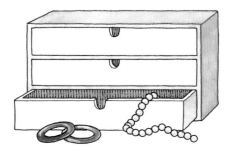

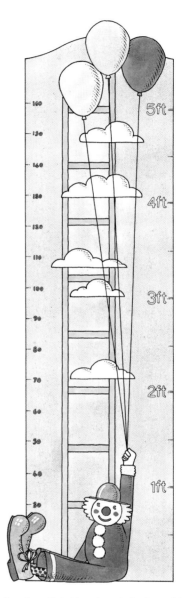

Another finishing touch that could be gleaned from garage storage is to firmly glue lids of screw-top jars to the underside of a low shelf. The jars will then screw into the lids and display their contents, such as craft items. A girl of this age will enjoy having a box or a pretty case for her first necklaces, bracelets and hair decorations. A box with tiny pull-out drawers for odds and ends or for collected treasures can sit on or near the table top, as well as a rack or shoebox to hold cassettes.

# An eight-year-old's room

The eight-year-old is a much more mature being, yet one who still needs to play. Board games, hobbies, simple needlework and construction kits will have taken over from earlier toys, and organized physical games and sports from unstructured rough and tumble. A computer may be on the horizon, or already installed, as well as other serious pieces of equipment such as microscope, telescope or chemistry set. Ideas about equipping their room may be advancing as well: your offspring might like to incorporate her own television, record player or dartboard. How far you go along with these requests depends on your general philosophy, of course, but whatever you feel about the right way to equip your child's room, you will realize that he or she will already be treating it much more seriously.

## Decorative ideas

If you have always wanted to give the windows or bed the full decorative treatment with cornice, swags and tie-backs, now will be the age that such a luxury will be truly appreciated, rather than seen as a good place for hide-and-seek. Good carpet could now be laid, in the knowledge that less sticky messes will be spilled on it. Few children will now be too nervous to clamber up to the ceiling to a platform bed, if you have always seen this as the answer to a space problem.

Letting the children have their say in the room's decoration will be excellent for their confidence building, and make them feel that their room really is their own place. Discussions about decoration will be rather more rational, too, though some children are frankly still rather likely to see your ideas about a nice cream wall with a delicate stencil border as dull, next to their own idea of a Ghostbusters motif paper with a dartboard hung up!

If you yearn for an old-fashioned look, try taking them to visit old houses that are open to the public where such children's rooms can be seen, and see

if the quaintness wins them over. Or do a little stencilling as a surprise: it may make them enthusiastic for more. But be realistic: a quaint room may simply be inappropriate for some modern children who would be much better off with a desk especially built to take a computer and its equipment than with an old-fashioned school desk that wasn't built for the job. Remember too that quite a lot of children are cautious and suspicious of the unknown, or even determined not to like the sound of what they hear. Only you can really judge sensitively

whether decorating your child's room as a complete surprise will be a success or a disaster. You don't want to ride roughshod over their feelings, nor let them miss a pleasant opportunity.

However much you take your child's choices into consideration, it will be important to decorate around the temperament of your child. At this age the sex of a child will be more clearly reflected in the decorative scheme of their room too. Obviously, you would think twice before putting up frilly curtaining for a boy who doesn't like

item of decoration she has previously treasured is now babyish or "yuk;" it is all part of growing up. Conversely, you may find that they wish to cling on to the nursery lampshade or keep their baby chair for a stuffed toy or doll to sit in because they are fond of the memories of the past. Don't try to force them out of this nostalgia.

Children of this age may enjoy quite strong colors on their walls. Even if you choose a wallpaper with an all-over design, it may be best to leave one wall painted or papered in a plain color, free of patterned paper. From this age onwards they will probably wish to make their own mark with posters, charts and all manner of, to them, fascinating material about baseball teams, dinosaurs or whatever the flavor of the month is; if these are stuck over patterned wallpaper it will make for rather a messy sight.

**Integrated storage**
It is likely that storage and work space will assume a dominant role from now on. Eight-year-olds have much more ability to command space with their constructions, whether of a home-made puppet theater or a major railway or road works stuck to hardboard and complete with carefully assembled accessories. Their wardrobe needs will grow too, with smarter dresses, long trousers and jackets and perhaps school uniform and sports gear. Bookshelf space will also be in demand, even if it is used for board games as much as for books.

It is important that the decorative theme of the room is done in such a way as to keep this increased storage provision looking uniform and not too shabby. You could perhaps paint all the shelving one clear color and cover the worktop in a modern, exciting colored laminate. Or you could install additional shelving and cupboards in a stylish birch-faced plywood or medium density fiberboard, which is easily worked and will take a variety of decorative treatments. Ensure that the storage fits in with the room as a whole.

*Above The computer co-exists with the teddy at this age. Open storage and wall displays add decoration.*

*Right An older child will be safe in a platform bed which frees floor space for games or storage. Ensure that any such construction is sturdily built.*

fussiness, but plenty of girls don't like fussiness and too many frills either, and would rather have a bright, plain blind. Don't be offended if your eight-year-old suddenly declares that some

■ See pages 40-41 *for planning an older child's room*

# Eight years and older

If you have been able to plan your child's room in step with her needs, you hopefully won't ever have felt defeated by the utter chaos or dinginess of her room, or had to turn down the request to have a friend to stay because there was nowhere the friend could sleep comfortably. For the future, too, you will want to continue seeing your child playing and working happily and concentratedly in her room. There may come a point when you realize she is living with hangovers from the past, which are cluttering up space that could be used for her present needs. Have a negotiated clear-out at this stage.

If you have hitherto avoided carpet, you may feel she is now old enough to treat it with respect; conversely, if you have installed carpet as a comfortable floor covering for little ones to sit on, and it is now showing its age, you could do away with it and switch to a polished floor with rugs. The rugs can easily be inexpensive Greek flokatis, pretty Indian dhurries or colorful rag rugs, all of which are washable and therefore a practical choice.

Check the state of your child's mattress, before she gets into her teens. If you have spent a few years with her sleeping in a second-hand bunk bed or an old family divan, this may be a good time to invest in a bed with a sturdy, well-made mattress that will see your child through the remaining years at home.

## Home study

If your child is likely to have quite a bit of homework and quiet study over the next ten years, consider investing in a decent, adjustable office-type chair or one of the adjustable chair-stools designed to keep a child's back at a good angle. Good posture now may save back problems later in life. Your child will enjoy the fun of casters,

*Right* Mementoes from nursery days are a reassuring part of a child's life and blend in with more sophistication.

*Below* Eye-catching graphics can be put to good use on the wall of an older child's room.

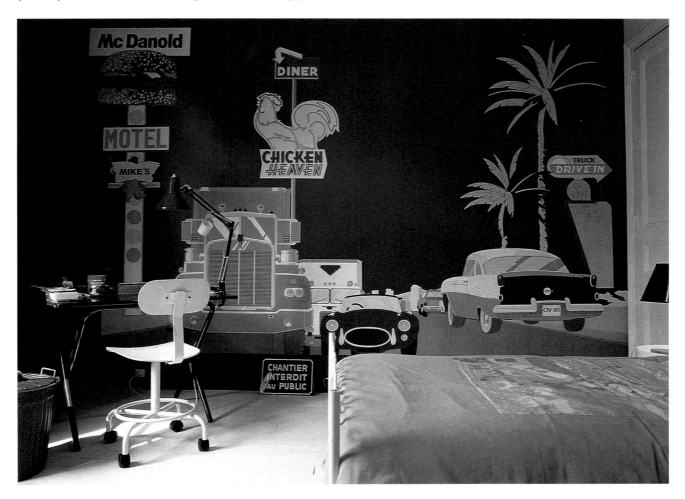

swivelling and moving the seat up and down and the chair-back forwards and backwards. Such a chair can be seen as an investment, in use for a great many years, and hopefully preventing any round shoulders and hunching.

In time, a larger desk may be a good idea. If there is not a lot of money to spend, look at second-hand office furniture – old wooden desks can be renovated or painted and give a good expanse of work surface.

### Increased storage
Looking to the future, make sure that there is enough of the right kind of

storage and worktop space for the coming years, which will probably bring record and other collections, more complicated hobbies and pursuits and piles of homework. You may have to provide a bookcase extension (perhaps you bought a system which could be added to in the first place) or add different shelving, repainting the whole lot to make it look homogenous.

The next few years will also see an ever-expanding wardrobe. You may need to build in a hanging rail, or re-install the wardrobe rail you removed years ago to make more shelf space for

a baby's needs. This may necessitate making more general storage elsewhere in the room.

Some girls will appreciate a dressing table: if you don't want to buy a brand new wooden one, clever disguises can be made. A round side table can be draped with fabric, held in place with a glass table top with ground, smooth edges. A mirror can be fixed to the wall just above it, or a free-standing small mirror placed on top of it. The wall mirror could be surrounded with small round screw-in bulbs, Hollywood style. Victorian or Edwardian wash stands can be similarly adapted.

■ See pages 108-109 *for making a mural*

# Finishing touches

Children from the age of eight or so onwards will appreciate all manner of decorative items from other countries. Indonesian shadow puppets, Indian felt and sequinned shapes and Chinese masks are all fascinating to a child who is really beginning to understand about travel and other cultures. Besides pictures and posters, consider more unusual things for hanging on the wall. These could include patchwork or appliquéed quilts or fabric wallhangings such as embroideries or decorative rugs.

Kites are another item that look splendid spread across a wall, especially the Chinese ones made of tissue paper, which are too fragile to

*Big, sturdy and bright hooks are a feature in themselves, but especially when used to hang colorful items.*

fly in any case. A large world map, fixed to a wall, will be both decorative and educational at the same time. Or a globe could be installed, possibly an illuminated one.

By now, children are old enough to construct their own finishing touches, so you could work out or choose a stencil pattern or mural together and, after some practice, allow her to apply it. Block-printing or sponging pictures on is another fairly simple technique that children can help with and this can be done on fabric as well as walls or furniture, so curtains or cushions could be decorated.

Musical children might welcome practicing space in their own room,

with a correctly sized chair if they play sitting down, and a music stand. A mirror may be a useful accessory to install now, if the room doesn't already have one, because children become more aware of their appearance around this age. A mirror will also reflect light from the windows and help to make the room seem lighter.

Look at the cupboard and door handles with a critical eye. They are a detail often overlooked, but a set of matching, contrasting colored knobs or D handles, in wood or a good quality plastic or porcelain, will make a lot of difference to the room's appearance. Good-looking handles could be a smart finishing note to the room as a whole.

# KNOW HOW

# DECORATING TECHNIQUES

You don't have to employ a professional to decorate your child's room: repairing, painting and wallpapering are well within most parents' abilities, even if you have never tackled this kind of task before. The trick is to understand what you have to do before you start doing it, which means reading through all of the explanations (preferably at least twice) before you pick up a paintbrush, and to plan ahead by buying, borrowing or hiring the right equipment. Provided you carry out the preparation thoroughly, you will find the decorating gets done magically.

# Preparing walls/1

No matter how much money you have spent on beautiful wallpaper and exactly the right shade of paint, if you do not apply it to surfaces which have been properly prepared and which are now clean and dry, you might as well throw it away. The job will not look good; and at worst you may even have problems with peeling wallpaper or flaking paint or mold coming through.

The idea of preparation sounds rather dull, because people think of it as a chore that must be done before the real creative work. Try thinking of it in a different way – as the rehearsal, without which the final performance would be embarrassingly bad. Approach it with enthusiasm, for every extra bit you do will make the end result that much better.

Inspect the walls, woodwork and ceiling of your child's room before you plan your decoration scheme – the state they are in may affect your plans. If the walls exhibit any form of mold – black spots or a webby kind of growth – don't try and decorate until you have discovered whether this has been caused by the use of an impermeable wall covering, such as vinyl paper, or by something more serious such as damp penetration or dry rot. You may need professional help to track it down.

The first thing you must establish is whether the plaster is sound. If when you knock the plaster with your knuckles on what you know to be a solid wall (gypsum board always sounds hollow), it sounds hollow or feels loose or spongy, it may need to be replaced. If the walls are already uneven or covered with a relief wallpaper, such as woodchip, it would be reasonable to expect a problem – the plaster may come away with the wall covering. If your budget does not run to replastering, and the paper is fixed securely, you may prefer to leave it in position (provided it does not have too bumpy a relief pattern on it). In this case you will probably be limited to simple repainting, though if you wish to paper the room you may be able to

use the existing wallpaper as lining paper if there is only one layer of it and it is firmly stuck down. But you will never be able to achieve a successful finish on crumbling plaster, and if you try to put up shelving or pictures, the screws won't stay in place and may fall out, bringing plaster with them.

Lumps and bumps may just mean that the walls have not been properly sanded and finished, which is a job that you can tackle. And replastering need not necessarily mean the whole room, but just filling in any holes or cracks and making smooth the parts that are not in a good state, which you can also do yourself. But if there is a sizeable area needing replastering, call in a professional plasterer, rather than trying to fill it with a proprietary brand of filler. As a general rule, if the holes are too large for a proprietary filler, they should be considered too large to be tackled by an amateur.

## Preparing the room

It is much easier to work in an empty room. If there is serious preparation to be done, move the furniture out and take up carpet. If the preparation work is light, it may be enough to pile the furniture in the center of the room and cover it with dust sheets. If you have to wait for newly-filled walls to dry, plan to be getting on with something else in the meantime.

Arrange for young children to camp out in another room, or even with neighbors or relations for a few days if you can. They may enjoy helping with the general destruction of paper stripping, and if you can use them to wet paper without causing a flood, or to strip without gouging holes in the wall, fine. But if you are stripping off woodwork paint that may have contained lead, they should be kept out of the way, since lead is dangerous to children, and gloss paint stripping equipment is potentially dangerous.

Consult the chart opposite to see how to treat the various surfaces that you are likely to encounter.

## SAFETY

△  *Turn off electricity at the electric box before wetting walls; but avoid wetting switches and outlets in any case. Cover with tape or polyethylene while wetting walls.*

△  *Stand only on a stable surface such as a spread stepladder or a solid trestle. Do not stretch out too far, risking overbalancing, and wear flat, non-slip-soled shoes.*

△  *Try and work in daylight or with a good source of electric light, unless you are doing something which requires switching off the electricity.*

△  *When using power tools, always switch off and disconnect before changing parts. Use a circuit breaker and check whether you need an extension cord. Always work with the cord out of the way, preferably behind you.*

△  *Wear protective goggles when sanding or chipping plus a face mask for excessively dusty work.*

△  *Always keep your fingers behind a tool's cutting edge.*

△  *Beware of inhaling fumes when dealing with chemical strippers; make sure the room is ventilated. Wear protective gloves which cover the wrists.*

△  *Don't work with asbestos. Call in an expert if you discover any (it is a fibrous-looking material with a blue or grey powdery surface).*

△  *Don't put leftovers of chemicals into food or drink containers which may be mistaken for the real thing.*

△  *Do not repaint with lead paint.*

△  *If you are stripping very old paintwork which may have had lead in it, don't use a blowtorch, which causes fumes, or a dry sander, which spreads the particles as dust, but use wet wet-and-dry paper, a chemical stripper or a hot-air paint stripper. Dispose of paint debris in the trash, not by burning, and wash your hands afterwards, especially before eating.*

## SURFACE PREPARATION

| Previous surface | New surface | Treatment |
|---|---|---|
| One layer ordinary paper | Paint (latex) | Check whether firmly stuck down. Can use as a base paper provided colors don't bleed (test small area first). If loose or if colors bleed, strip. May need several coats to cover, especially if pattern is bright. |
|  | Paper | Can use as base lining if firmly stuck down. But make sure new paper overlaps old seams, doesn't match them. |
| Layers of paper | Anything | Strip completely. |
| Plastic-surfaced paper | Anything | Strip. May be dry strippable in which case peel off carefully, leaving base behind. Possible to paint over some paper-backed vinyl, but test an area if you want to try before going ahead. |
| Metallized paper | Paint | Check whether firmly stuck down. Paint undercoat with aluminum paint sealer. |
|  | Paper | Strip. |
| Relief/woodchip paper | Anything | Strip. |
| Distemper/white-wash | Anything | Wash and scrape off. |
| Latex paint | Paint | Wash thoroughly, rub down and repair damaged areas. Rub down till smooth, then wash the wall again. |
|  | Paper | Wash, and seal with size, thinned wallpaper paste or another coat of thinned latex. If using vinyl paper, use fungicidal paste. |
| Old plaster | Anything | Rub down thoroughly, especially to remove efflorescence caused by salts leaking from old paper. Repair plaster as necessary. If plaster not an especially good surface, may be best to line wall with lining paper – cross-line (i.e. horizontally not vertically) if you are then going to paper it. |
| New plaster | Latex | Wait for at least two weeks, then sand lightly, and use thinned latex as undercoat. |
|  | Paper wall covering | After 6 months apply size and/or a dilute coat of latex, then wallpaper. |
|  | Vinyl paper | Use after minimum 6 months, with fungicidal paste. |
| Metal radiators, pipes and window frames | Paint | Clean; rub down, using adhesive paper or chemical stripper, not a blowtorch which could damage metal. Remove all traces of any rust with a wire brush and cut away rusted areas (if pipes or radiators are this bad, they will obviously need to be repaired or replaced professionally). Treat with rust inhibitor and metal primer – choose correct primer for type of metal – except for brass and copper which need no priming. Then paint with oil-based or special metal paint. Aluminum does not need painting, but can be if you prefer a painted finish. |

# Preparing walls/2

Stripping old surfaces is the first stage of preparing a room for redecoration. Old wallpaper may need to be removed, and paintwork in poor condition should first be either stripped or sanded down.

## Stripping wallpaper

If you are dealing with a dry strippable or easy-strip vinyl-coated paper, your task is relatively easy. To check whether it is an easy-strip paper, lift a corner and pull gently: it will simply come away in a long strip. Walk backwards, pulling the paper towards you. Easy-strip papers generally leave their lining behind them, which forms an excellent, though sometimes rather absorbent, coat for whatever you want to do next. Unfortunately, if some of this backing paper comes away, you had better try and remove it all – it may be unstable and will leave ridges where missing patches occur.

With all other wallpapers, you will probably have to use water to soften the paste or glue which held the paper on. If there are several layers of paper, or thick paper which has been painted over, or you are dealing with washable paper designed to repel water, you have a harder task to get to the bottom layer of paste. To speed this up, score the paper with a serrated scraper or a nail-studded piece of wood. Alternatively, slash it with a utility knife, or use a wire brush or a grit-surfaced abrasive paper, before soaking with warm water and scraping. You will need to tackle painted relief papers with particular energy in this way. Beware of getting water into electrical apparatus such as behind a light switch or outlet – turn electricity off at the electricity box before you start.

The best kind of scraper for stripping wallpaper is a thin, flat one with a wide blade – anything triangular is more likely to dig holes in the plaster. Push gently upwards, starting at the bottom and working up, and try and lift off pieces as large as possible. Spread

newspaper or plastic sheeting on the floor to catch the scraps. Alternatively, you can use a steam stripper to help you (these can be hired).

Once all the paper is off, allow the wall to dry, and rub off any last particles of paper with abrasive paper. Then give the whole surface a wash with detergent solution. If any mold has developed as a result of an impermeable wall covering, treat the wall with a proprietary mold inhibitor or with a solution of household bleach diluted five to one with water.

## Stripping distemper and whitewash

You can recognize distemper by its flakiness and readiness to come away when you rub it with your finger. It is rarely found in recently-built houses. Distemper has to be thoroughly removed, since it will interact with new paint or wallpaper paste and prevent either adhering to the wall. Wash, scrub and scrape to remove distemper and whitewash completely from walls.

Ceiling moldings which have been

repeatedly whitewashed over or distempered a dozen times will need to be softened with plentiful applications of warm water. Adding sugar soap may help. Using a plant sprayer filled with warm water is easier than ladling water on with a sponge. Then gently dig away at the caked deposits with an awl or similar-shaped pointed tool: you want to remove the whitewash, not the plaster. It should gradually come off, sometimes in satisfying caked chunks, to reveal the pattern beneath.

## Stripping paint from woodwork

If there is just one layer of gloss or other oil-based paint on woodwork, and it is sound, you need only rub it down before repainting, using coarse-grade sandpaper. This will roughen the surface up slightly to enable new paint to adhere to it easily. If layers have built up, however, you should try to remove it: oil-based paint is thick and too many layers of it make for a rather lumpy finish.

Oil-based paint on woodwork can be stripped with a hot air stripper or

## TOOLBOX

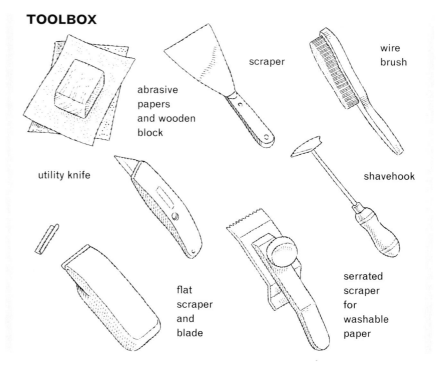

abrasive papers and wooden block

utility knife

flat scraper and blade

scraper

wire brush

shavehook

serrated scraper for washable paper

blowtorch, or with a chemical stripper, following the manufacturer's instructions. Chemical strippers tend to fall into two types: those based on solvents and those based on caustic soda. All stripping methods work by softening the paint till it blisters and lifts, at which point you remove it with a scraper. The two methods can also blister and lift your skin, and a blowtorch carries a risk of fire so they all have to be used with great caution. *Solvent strippers* are easy to apply and are especially useful for wood moldings and oddly-shaped surfaces.

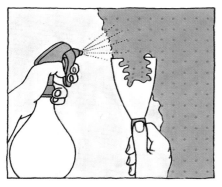

Softening with a plant sprayer is a good technique for wallpapers that are not dry-strippable or vinyl-coated, and for paint-caked plaster moldings. Use warm water.

An electric steam stripper is labor-saving for large areas. Soften the paper, then scrape upward with the flat edge of your tool. Wear a protective glove when using.

Solvents can be used on latex, cellulose and oil-based paints, although they don't work as well on polyurethane paints as on other glosses. They are thick and gooey, and should be applied by brush and left for no longer than the stated time (usually about eight to ten minutes) before being removed with a scraper.

The best way to work is to apply stripper to the first area, wait, apply it to the next area, then scrape the first area, apply stripper to the third area, scrape the second area, and so on. The "area" should be no bigger than you can scrape with a flat scraper or shavehook before the stripper dries.

Some strippers of this kind come with a kind of "blanket" to lay on top. These can be effective on flat surfaces, though they are not very good for fiddly areas. Cleaning the "blanket" for re-use can be difficult.

*Caustic strippers* come as a paste or in pellet form, which need dissolving in water before use. Unless the pellets have a built-in thickener, it is a good idea to add wallpaper paste to the mixture so the caustic sticks to what it is stripping, rather than running off. They are rather alarming to use since the chemical reaction makes them hot and they can spit; always add caustic to water, not the other way round, and never use it near children. The safest place to use these strippers is out of doors, but not where you want anything to grow; it is essential to wear protective clothing and goggles. Doors or shutters can be taken off their hinges to make it easier to strip them.

Caustic strippers can be used to strip latex and oil-based paints, but not other cellulose paints, and they tend to darken the natural color of wood. If you later want to stain the stripped wood, you will be better off avoiding this kind of stripper. You can apply it to large areas in one go, and leave it for a longer time – usually about two to four hours – but check how quickly the paint is dissolving after half an hour or you may over-strip.

Caustic soda pellets dissolved in water can be used to make a bath in which to strip whole doors, shutters and other wooden furniture – this is rather daunting done at home, but professional strippers will take your woodwork in. Since it is strongly alkaline, caustic will need to be thoroughly neutralized by undiluted vinegar afterwards, and then the item washed well and allowed to dry naturally, not too near heat. Since the caustic dissolves glue and dries out wood, however, the joints of wooden objects may need repairing afterwards.

A gas blowtorch is safer and easier to use than a Kerosene one, though it can burn badly if care is not taken. Wear a protective glove on the hand holding the scraper.

Apply chemical paint stripper to small sections, leave it to soften the paint and scrape off. Use with a shavehook (an angled scraper) for moldings.

# Preparing walls/3

*Blowtorch or hot air stripper* Kerosene blowtorches are cheap, but messy and awkward to use; gas blowtorches are more expensive but a lot simpler in use. Before you start work, place a sheet of non-flammable material below what you are stripping to catch hot paint shavings. Have a heat-impervious stand (such as a ceramic tile) ready nearby to stand the hot blowtorch on when you put it down. Wear thick gloves to protect your hands.

The method is to play the hot air jet or flame of the blowtorch over the surface to be stripped, keeping the machine about 6in (15cm) away. Work upward and keep the heat away from any glass. Hold a scraper in the other hand and push the softened paint off with this. You will probably be left with some paint residue which can be removed later by rubbing with abrasive paper or with fine steel wool (see Abrasive papers, below).

*Washing down* Finally, wash and rinse both wall and wood surfaces. Even if you have not needed to strip a sound surface, you must still wash it thoroughly. The aim is to remove household dirt and grease which would prevent new paint or wall-covering paste from properly adhering to the wall or properly drying out once it is there. Washing an unstripped surface means using detergent in warm water followed by rinsing with clean warm water, then allowing it to dry thoroughly. When washing a stripped surface, use warm water with a trace of vinegar in it.

## Stripping paint from walls

Unless you are anxious to get back to a bare surface, sound latex paint need only be washed down, unless it is clogging up moldings or has been applied over layers of paper.

For gloss paint used on a wall, wash, rinse and dry the wall, then rub the surface down with a coarse grade of sandpaper. Wipe over to remove the dust. Finally, seal with wallpaper paste, size or latex paint.

## Filling walls

Your aim is to make smooth all surfaces before any painting or papering. Making good is the term used to describe the various methods of filling cracks and holes. It can be a slow process, but will provide a uniform surface, ready to decorate.

Sand down and rake out any loose material, then moisten the surface well to ensure good adhesion. Fill (preferably overfill) any holes and cracks using a putty knife. Allow the

### TOOLBOX

orbital electric sander

putty knife

steel wool

sandpaper in three grades

filling to dry, then sand it. You may have to repeat the process several times, as filled areas subside slightly as they dry and what may seem smooth when wet is ridged at the edges when it has dried.

Deep cracks or holes will have to be filled in layers about ½-¾in (10-15mm) deep at a time, allowing the filler to dry in between layers. Use a good-quality proprietary filler, or if there are many areas to fill around the house, ask your local lumber yard to sell you a bulk bag of plaster.

You may in any case have to use plaster rather than filler for larger cracks and holes. The plaster is mixed to a smooth, thick consistency with water and applied with a plasterer's trowel. Bear in mind, however, that plastering is a tricky skill and it might be a good idea to call in some professional help if there are a number of large holes.

Fine cracks in gypsum board partition walls may be better treated with a thick textured paint because the best fillers to achieve the right kind of surface finish are too rigid and will probably just crack again.

## Sanding

Large areas are more comfortably done with an electric sander. The abrasive paper fitted to it could be sandpaper (sometimes called glasspaper) or, both more expensive but longer-lasting and less likely to clog up, aluminum oxide and waterproof silicon carbide. The latter is often called "wet and dry" and when it is used wet (and the surface it is rubbing is made wet too) it lasts for a very long time, but causes the material removed to stick to the surface which is being rubbed down. To remove the debris, you must wash the surface down thoroughly. Wet and dry paper can be washed to free any material clogging its surface.

When using an electric sander, beware of the disc sander which leaves circular marks that are difficult to remove. This may not matter if you are

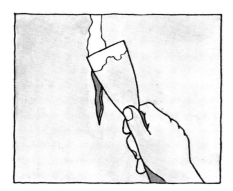

Filling cracks in walls can be done with powder or a ready-mixed filler. Fill the crack or small hole proud (i.e. slightly raised), and leave to dry thoroughly.

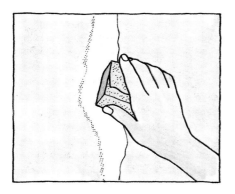

Sanding the dried filler flush with the surface is best done with sandpaper wrapped around a cork or wooden block or with a purpose-made sponge sanding block.

going to paint the wood, but even so, if it is done with too heavy a hand, it will leave a circular texture. An orbital sander may leave less noticeable swirls, which can be readily erased by hand sanding.

*Abrasive papers* Abrasive papers are sold as sheets (normally 11½in by 9in, approximately 275mm by 225mm), graded according to their coarseness or grit size. A number will be marked on the back of the sheet. For sandpaper, aluminum oxide and waterproof silicon carbide, the higher the number, the finer the grade (from

12 to 600, with 600 being the finest).

There may be another difference, according to whether the abrasive particles are very close together ("close coat") or wider apart ("open coat"). Open coat papers are slower to clog than close ones. For some electric sanders, you will need special size sanding discs.

When rubbing down walls or woodwork, choose a grade appropriate to the amount of material to be removed. Start with a coarse grade and work up to a fine one, but always beware of choosing a grade that is too coarse to start with or you will damage wood moldings, or take off too much newly-laid plaster.

### Preparing wood

New wood, for example if you have replaced baseboards, will need priming before you apply paint. The same applies to any areas of paintwork which have been chipped to expose an expanse of bare wood.

Wood that has been stripped may have obvious flaws. If it is to be painted over, you need only fill holes with plastic wood or spackle, sand it well down and then prime it. Any knots exposed in the wood should be treated with patent knotting (this can be bought in small cans) before priming. Allow the patent knotting to dry thoroughly before applying the primer to the wood.

Beware of rubbing down wood too smoothly, with a superfine grade of steel wool or abrasive paper, if it is to be painted or stained: this may have the effect of polishing the wood, making it difficult for the grain to accept its next coat. It is better to apply primer and one coat of paint, then rub the wood down finely, clearing off the dust thoroughly, before applying the top coat of paint to it.

If you wish to stain or varnish wood, you may have to tint any wood filler or plastic wood with a wood stain or a touch of artists' oil paint. If any knots have fallen out, replacing them with a

Use an electric orbital sander to sand large areas if you want to remove paint completely, and return to the original wood. A disc sander may leave marks.

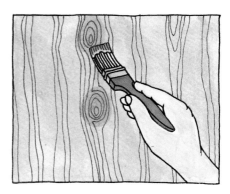

It is important to paint knots in new or newly exposed wood with patent knotting. This prevents knots drying, shrinking and falling out and also stops the resin oozing.

glued-in section of wooden dowel may look more natural than using either a commercial wood filler or plastic wood.

If rubbing down wooden surfaces by hand, you could either wrap the abrasive paper around a rectangular wooden or cork block or buy a ready-made block, generally made of sponge, which is usually coated with different grades of either aluminum oxide or silicon carbide on each side. Alternatively you could use steel wool in the correct grade for the condition of the wood.

# Painting walls/1

After the slow work of preparation, the painting stage comes as a great relief, but should not be rushed through. If you rush it too much you may end up with visible brush strokes, paint-spattered baseboards and dust or bristles trapped in the dry paint.

First, select the method of painting you prefer – brush, roller or paint pad. Unless you have decided to paint the walls in a shiny-finished, tough, oil-based gloss paint, you will probably be using a latex or eggshell paint. These paints are water based, so the equipment you use with them can easily be washed out in water after use.

## Paintbrush method

Applying paint with a brush is uncomplicated, but may be rather slow for covering a large room. You will have to use a brush if you are painting heavy, textured wallpaper, in order to get into the recessed shapes.

Paintbrushes are available in different widths. For walls, a 4in (100mm) brush will be wide enough to cover space quickly; anything smaller is more suitable for woodwork, while a wider (6in/150mm) brush may be too tiring to work with – full of paint, it is quite heavy to control. You will also need a narrower "cutting-in" brush, generally with angled bristles, for filling in the edges next to doors and windows where a large brush cannot be maneuvered easily.

When buying brushes, avoid the very cheapest, even if you never mean to paint again; they may lose bristles quickly, which will be irritatingly trapped in the paintwork, and short, coarse synthetic-fiber filaments do not give good results. The most expensive brushes are best avoided also: these are for professionals, and need quite a bit of "breaking-in." Choose middle-priced brushes with a bevelled edge to the bristles. Bristles with "flagged" (split) ends help the paint to go on as smoothly as possible.

You will also need a paint bucket – a wide-topped plastic or metal container

with a handle, into which you can pour paint from the can. It is easier to carry about than a heavy can, prevents any "bits" that may get into the paint from messing up the whole canful, and means that you can mix the paints from two cans when painting a large room to prevent any slight color change between the two tins being at all noticeable.

## Roller method

A roller is a handle with a frame on to which a sleeve, the part you paint with, is fixed. It is probably easier to use a roller than a brush in a large room since it will cover more of the wall at a time. The sleeves can be made from a variety of materials: foam, sheepskin, synthetic fiber and woolpile.

When choosing a roller, check whether sleeves can be replaced, and how easy this is to do. Again, it might be best to avoid the very cheapest rollers, which are usually made of foam. Though in some people's hands they produce reasonable results, they

tend to hold too much paint, which then drips, throw off a fine spray of paint as you work and can leave small bubbles in the paint surface, which dry quickly. Foam sleeves work better with gloss paints. On the whole, a smooth wall surface demands a smooth surfaced roller (mohair or a short wool or synthetic pile), and a more textured surface a shaggier roller (sheepskin or a longer synthetic pile). Mohair gives a fine result with latex or oil-based paint, while sheepskin is not suitable for oil-based paints.

You will also need a roller tray, made of plastic or metal, with a deeper end into which to pour the paint and a sloping, ridged end over which to draw the loaded roller to take off excess paint. You will still need an edging or "cutting-in" brush, since rollers cannot paint right up to the wall, window or door edges. You can buy extension handles for high walls and ceilings, and special radiator and pipe rollers to enable you to get the roller down behind these fixtures.

## TOOLBOX

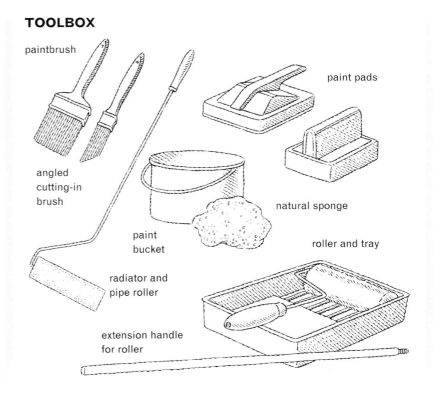

paintbrush

angled cutting-in brush

paint bucket

radiator and pipe roller

extension handle for roller

paint pads

natural sponge

roller and tray

## Paint pads

Paint pads have a handle, a thin layer of foam on a backing plate and a top layer of mohair for painting. They are normally square or rectangular, though there is an increasing range of shapes, including triangular "touch-up" pads, and they come in a range of sizes from around 2½in by 2in (65mm by 50mm) up to 9in by 4in (230mm by 100mm) for walls. Like rollers, they need a tray which has a narrower, slightly deeper paint compartment with a lip or (better) a roller for scraping the paint-loaded pad over (sometimes necessary to put the paint on evenly). Results with latex paint can be very good and even, and they are generally splash-free. However, some people find large pads tiring to use – you have to dip just the pile, not the foam, into the paint, which can be tricky, and paint until the pad drags on the wall, which is laborious. Results with gloss paint and on textured surfaces are less good. If you can't find angled pads for edges, use cutting-in brushes. Because they are difficult to clean, disposable paint pads may be the best buy.

## Before starting work

The most important thing to avoid when painting is dust. Even if you have just finished stripping the surfaces, wash them down before painting and, once they have dried, rub them over with a clean, lint-free (not fluffy) cloth. Make sure the floor is swept and the baseboards and windows clean. Cover the floor with a non-slip plastic sheet or dust sheets. If it is difficult to roll back a wall-to-wall carpet, cover the edges with wide sticky tape as well. Remove free-standing wall fixtures. Before opening the paint can, wipe the top to remove any dust or particles, and make sure that the paint bucket or paint tray is completely clean.

If you are using new brushes, wash them out in warm soapy water first, then rinse them, to soften the bristles and shake out any that may be loose. Dry thoroughly by shaking. Check old

brushes to make sure they won't smear your new paint with an old color. Flap the brushes backward and forward across your hand to remove dust and loose bristles.

The order of work is described fully on the following pages.

## Finishing off

It is very important to clean and store painting equipment properly. Do not leave brushes and rollers lying around until they dry and do not leave them standing upright in water until "later." Leaving them standing can distort brush bristles and soak them so full of water that whatever you dip them into next will be excessively runny. If you take a short break, wrap the painting implement in polyethylene, with a

*Sponging adds depth to the paint color and gives an attractive finish which is not difficult to achieve.*

rubber band around it to secure it.

When you have finished, wipe your painting implements backwards and forwards across dry paper to remove as much paint as possible (but don't stub them down, which will damage them). If you have been using latex paint, wash the implements well in warm soapy water, with plenty of rinses, using your fingers to work right to the base of the bristles.

Store carefully too: wrap brushes and roller sleeves in paper towels with their bristles in the right shape, and lay them flat in a drawer or cupboard.

# Painting walls/2

The best light for painting in is clear, bright daylight, but without too strong a sun dazzling you and casting shadows to confuse you. Obviously, not every day can be like this, but make sure that window coverings are removed and, if painting in the evening, use a high wattage bulb with no shade over it.

If you are decorating a whole room the order of painting should be ceiling first, followed by walls and finally the woodwork. If you are papering the walls, paint the ceiling first, then the woodwork and finally do the wallpapering.

When painting with a brush, paint should be applied in horizontal strokes, over an imaginary square area on the wall, starting in a top corner of the room and moving along and down, then the wet painted area lightly brushed upwards (or downwards near the ceiling) to make it smooth before moving on to the next brushful. When painting with a roller or paint pad, apply paint in broad strips from the ceiling to the floor, using criss-cross strokes down the length of each strip.

Whichever implement you are using, your aim is to keep a wet edge to the paint so that as new paint goes on, it can be brushed into the paint already on the wall. Modern latex paints are generally very good, but there is always a danger that if an edge has been allowed to dry, where you start painting again will show as a slight ridge or a distinct line when the paint dries. To avoid patchy-looking painting, never stop for a break in the middle of a wall, but finish it to the edges first.

## Order of work

■ Tip a quantity of paint into your working container and replace the lid tightly on the can. If you will be using two or more cans, halfway through the first can, open the second and mingle the paints to avoid any color change from one can to the next.
■ Paint the edges of a wall first, including around the window and door

## PAINTING PROCEDURE

Always start painting a large, flat area of wall at its edges: around a door and window frame, along a baseboard and against a ceiling. Paint a wall all in one go.

Paint the ceiling first, then walls and finally woodwork. If you want to sand the floor, do this before painting; lay carpet or other flooring afterwards.

Use an angled "cutting-in" brush or specially shaped paint pad to help achieve clean, straight edges along door and window frames, and baseboards.

Paint pads are an alternative to a brush or roller. Do not overload them with paint, and keep the surface of the pad flat on the wall at all times.

frames and the baseboard edge, in a strip about 2in (5cm) wide, using a narrow or angled cutting-in brush.

When you approach with your larger brush, roller or pad, you will be able to "feather" new paint into this strip, without it touching the edges.
■ Begin painting walls in the corner nearest the window, working away from the light. Complete one whole coat of the room and allow it to dry before starting a second coat. You will certainly need a second coat, at least,

and possibly even a third for a good final finish, which can be sponged down to remove dirty marks. Keep a wet cloth handy in case you spill, spray or splash, and clean up immediately.
■ The very first coat will act as a primer and, for plaster walls being painted with latex paint, the "primer" can be a water-thinned layer of the actual paint you are using. This does not seal the wall in the sense of allowing nothing through it, but "settles" the wall surface.

■ Metal surfaces such as radiators and pipes must be given an appropriate primer and painted with one or two coats of oil-based paint, using a radiator brush, roller or pad.

## Sponging

Sponging gives an attractive finish which beginners can easily tackle. In fact, sponging offers a choice of two finishes, according to whether you sponge the paint on or sponge it off, and it can be done with latex paint or with an oil glaze. The latex will give a more opaque, milky, soft effect; the glaze a more lustrous one.

You need one or two medium-sized natural sea sponges and a supply of newspaper. The walls which are to be sponged should first be painted, either with latex if you want to sponge in latex, or with oil-based matte eggshell if you are to sponge in glaze or an oil-based paint. The glaze is obtained by mixing ready-bought oil glaze (which looks a creamy yellow in the can but is transparent when thinned) with turpentine, half and half.

Then comes the exciting part of adding the color, which is artists' oil color (bought in tubes from art shops). To get the color right, use a small amount of the mixed oil glaze with a proportionately small amount of artists' oil. Mix the oil with turpentine in a clean glass jar first, in order to get it a suitable adding consistency. If you are using a pale artists' oil, however, mix it with white eggshell paint first in order to stop the yellowing linseed oil in the glaze altering the color. This may mean that you will lose the translucency of a pure glaze.

Experiment until you like the color, then mix enough in the same proportions to cover the area to be sponged – about half as much as for one coat of ordinary paint. The final mixture should be approximately the thickness of cream.

*To sponge on*, squeeze the sponge out in clean water until it is soft but not dripping wet, just damp. Dip it into

## SPONGING ON

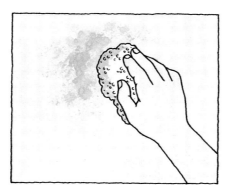

**1** Dip a damp natural sponge into the prepared color and dab it evenly over the wall; soften it with another damp sponge if the edges seem too definite.

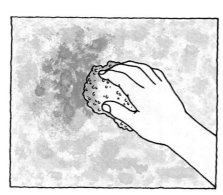

**2** To achieve a prettily dappled effect, apply the glaze or wash in a second color; you can do this before the first sponged-on color is dry.

some of the glaze poured into a paint tray and test on newspaper. If you are happy with the color and texture produced, start dabbing the sponge evenly over the wall. If the effect seems too definite, soften it with a clean wet sponge, or one wrung out in an even more diluted color.

You can put on a second layer while the first is still wet; the second color will be the dominant one.

*To sponge off*, paint is applied with a brush, then taken off with a sponge.

The base coats should be applied as normal, then an oil glaze, mixed and tinted as above, applied, to be dabbed off immediately with a wrung-out sponge. It is easier if two people do this, as fresh oil glaze should be applied while the first area is being sponged to prevent sharp drying lines showing. When the sponge is saturated, clean it in turpentine, then soapy water, followed by rinsing – you will need two sponges to do this.

## Colorwashing

This creates an attractive luminous surface, which, depending on the colors chosen, looks as appropriate in a cottage as in a rather smart child's room: the layers of paint means that there is something to look into in the wall surface. It looks good applied straight on bare plaster, even rather imperfect plaster, when it will make the room look as from a previous century. It makes a good background for stencils.

Paint the walls first with two coats of matte latex or oil-based eggshell paint. The latex will be better for a soft, milky look; the oil-based paint for a look with more sheen. Then paint over the top with either several coats of very thinned-down (as much as three to one of water to paint) water-based color on the latex, or oil-based paint (or a glaze made of artists' oils mixed about 60:40 with turpentine) on the eggshell. Allow to dry completely between each coat. These colorwash coats should be painted on with a soft, clean brush using a loose, slap-it-on style – it doesn't matter about seeing the brush marks since that is the idea. But avoid drips and messy brush marks: the effect should be freehand, but evenly executed.

To create an even softer effect, use a clean, dry cotton rag to wipe off some of the top coats. As for colors, pale ones look best on a light base, and top colors should be the same tone as the base layer. Seal latex colorwashing with a clear matte varnish which will make it washable.

# Stencilling walls

An increasing number of people are trying their hands at stencilling as a way of individualizing rooms, adding inexpensive decoration and giving a room a charming, old-fashioned look in a contemporary way. Almost any surface can be stencilled on, but appropriateness is really the key. Stencilling is a very old technique, and has been used in many circumstances, but it would be a waste to put it where it has to fight for attention with several other patterns and details.

You can make your own stencil or buy a ready-made one or even books of them (you may have to treat the pages of these, to make them firm enough for use). Some stencils are designed especially for children. The basic principle of stencilling is to paint a picture on a wall through a frame. The stencil itself enables exactly the same design to be repeated, to make a frieze, a border or a random pattern. Different colors can be used, or just

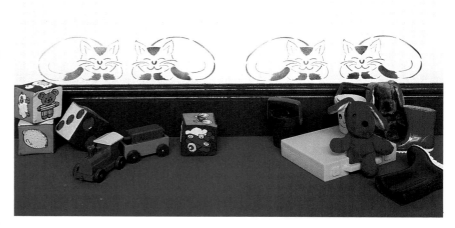

*Stencilling is an effective and inexpensive way of adding decoration to a plain paint finish. These stencilled cats lend a witty touch to a plain white wall. Their colors blend in with the room's overall color scheme as well as with children's primary-colored toys and accessories.*

one. The most important points to remember when stencilling are that very little color is needed, and that the stencil must stay firmly in place.

## Stencilling equipment

You need material from which to cut the stencil, a surface to cut on, a cutting tool, masking tape to fix the stencil, color or paint, and a brush.
*Stencil* This can be thin card, but stencil paper (oiled manila) or a flexible acetate such as Mylar is more durable.
*Drawing materials* If you are making your own design, you will need to draw it out first. A suitable shape to stencil has distinct "open" and "closed" areas, the closed areas acting as "bridges" to hold the stencil together and to make plain spaces between the colors. Once drawn, you can transfer the design to stencil paper by tracing over the original, then drawing firmly over the tracing to impress the design on to the stencil paper. If you use acetate, you have to draw the lines with a metal-nibbed pen such as a Rapidograph, or you could score the design through tracing paper with a sharp point.
*Cutting board and knife* A special cutting board or piece of hardboard is needed. Small flexible craft knives with sharp, disposable blades are best.
*Brushes* The traditional stencil brush comes in different sizes and is

## EQUIPMENT

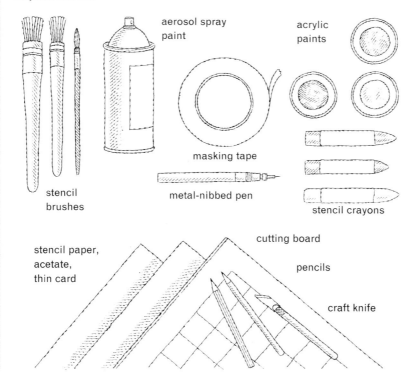

stencil brushes

aerosol spray paint

acrylic paints

masking tape

metal-nibbed pen

stencil crayons

stencil paper, acetate, thin card

cutting board

pencils

craft knife

## CUTTING AND APPLYING A STENCIL

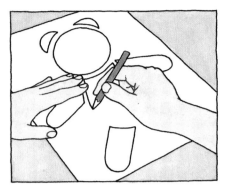

**1** Choose simple designs when starting to stencil, remembering to leave "bridges" between the parts that will be cut out. Use card, stencil paper or acetate.

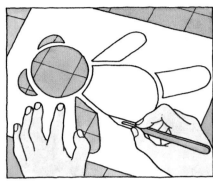

**2** Cut out the stencil template carefully with a sharp craft knife. Fix or hold the stencil firmly on a cutting board or hardboard while cutting.

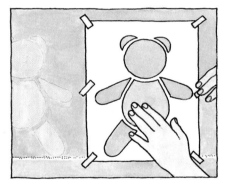

**3** Fix the stencil on the wall with masking tape, making sure it is straight and that there are no gaps behind which paint could ooze out.

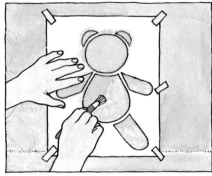

**4** Dab very small amounts of stencil paint through the open parts of the stencil with a dry stencil brush, using "pouncing" or jabbing movements.

characterized by the shortness of the bristles. For small, detailed areas, a small artist's brush will be needed.
*Paint or crayons* Anything too thick or too thin or too slow-drying will be no good for stencilling because when the color is applied to the empty part of the stencil you want it to stay put, not ooze under the stencil frame or, when you remove the stencil, start to spread. Stencil crayons, which are not used directly but "painted" on a piece of manila paper and picked up from there

with a brush, are one possibility. Artists' acrylic paints are also good and so are special stencil paints, some of which are made to appear shaded. But many people use latex, aerosol spray paint, or children's ready-mixed poster or powder paints.
*Sundries* Masking tape is useful for fixing a stencil, for covering areas you do not wish to paint with a particular color and for screening nearby parts of the surface. Turpentine will be necessary if you are using oil-based

paint, plus paper towels for cleaning up and wiping brushes. For stencilled friezes you will need a carpenter's level and tape measure plus chalked string to make a straight line.

### Applying the stencil

Having bought or made the stencil, plan the colors you will use, trying them out first on plain paper. Before you apply them for real, practice the stencil method of putting a tiny amount of color on the brush, which should usually be a dry brush, and "pouncing" or jabbing a little color through the stencil on to the surface. Old saucers, plastic lids or jam jar lids can be used for holding paint. You want to color the surface, not saturate it, and the resultant unevenness is considered to be part of a stencil's appeal. The same goes for slightly blurred edges: stencilling is not a crisp art.

If you are working a design that calls for several colors, you could leave the stencil in place and apply each color one at a time, waiting for one to dry before going on to the next. Make sure that you have marked clearly which color belongs with each hole. Alternatively, you can move round the room, lifting the stencil and applying all of one color at a time. The advantage of this is that you can mix one amount of color at a time: fast-drying colors may simply dry up if you use the other method. If you can cut enough of an identical border, you could cover a surface quite quickly by sticking several sheets up at one time.

Another way to deal with several colors is to cut several stencils, each of which has only one color's part of the pattern cut out. Acetate, being transparent, is very good for this, because when you lay an acetate stencil down you can see immediately where it has to go in relation to the already painted parts of a pattern. If the stencil you are using is opaque you have to be extremely careful that you have lined it up correctly each time; registration marks on the wall will help.

■ See page 67 *for another example of stencilled walls*

# Painting murals

Painting a mural on the wall of your child's room is something very special and personal: it can't be bought in shops, and it will give you a great sense of pride. Even if you don't rate your artistic talents highly, you can get a good result with a little cheating.

Unless you feel able to tackle a mural freehand – that is, drawing or painting straight from your imagination on to the wall – you can use the squaring up method. This is the one to use if you are not totally confident of your artistic abilities. In either case, the wall surface should be clean, not at all flaky, and painted with either an oil-based paint, such as eggshell, on which you could paint the mural using oil or oil-based paints, or with water-based undercoat or latex, on which you could use latex paint or children's paints such as poster paints, ready-mixed liquid or powder paints. Artists' acrylics are a lovely medium, but might become expensive over a large area. However, you could make them go further by using them to tint ordinary latex paint or oil-based undercoat to the required color. You could use other expensive paints, such as oil paints or artist's gouache, in the same way. Experiment with small amounts first.

### Order of work
First decide on your subject. Suppose you decide to do an engine, as in the picture on this page. Look in children's books for an engine on which to base the shape of yours. Do the same for every element of the chosen "scene."
■ Trace over the outline with a fine, sharp pencil, and then lay the tracing face down over a sheet of graph paper, making sure that a leading edge of the drawing is lined up with a bold line on the graph paper. Pin the tracing down

with masking tape and go over the lines of the drawing with a sharp pencil to transfer the pencilled shape to the graph paper. Then draw over the marked outline again, to make the image quite clear.
■ The next step is to square up the wall or part of wall where the mural will go. Drawing squares on the wall, which correspond to the squares on the graph paper, will enable you to enlarge the design, but still draw it to the same scale. First measure two vertical lines from the ceiling down to the floor, on either side of the painting area, and make a light pencil mark. Stretch a long straight rule between the two marks at the top of the wall, making sure the line is true by using a

spirit level. Lightly join the two marks, and continue to draw horizontal lines down the wall, making them an equal distance apart, say 12in (30cm). To draw the verticals, measure 12in (30cm) along from the left-hand side and mark this distance on the top and bottom horizontal. Check that the line is true with a spirit level or plumbline, and join the two marks, using the straight edge or rule. Continue to work along to the right until your grid of squares is complete.
■ You must decide on the finished scale of the work. You can scale up from your graph paper sketch by making, say, a ¾in (2cm) graph-paper square correspond to one of the large 12in (30cm) squares, or scale up to a

*The mural in this child's bedroom has been taken over several walls, and clouds have even continued over the ceiling. An older child could help to execute the simpler elements of a mural.*

■ See pages 76 and 90 *for other examples of murals in children's rooms*

## MAKING A MURAL

**1** First plan and draw out your design on squared paper. Each square will correspond to a large wall square.

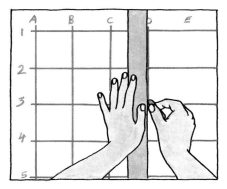

**2** Draw a matching, but scaled up, grid on the wall in chalk or other erasable medium; number and letter the squares.

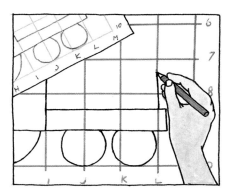

**3** Transfer the design from the graph paper to the wall grid, drawing on each wall square exactly what appears on each "blueprint" square.

lesser degree by making a 1½in (4cm) graph-paper square correspond to each 12in (30cm) square. To scale down, you would need to sub-divide one or more of the 12in (30cm) wall squares into smaller squares, and then make each, say, 1½in (4cm) graph-paper square equal to a ¾in (2cm) wall square. You would probably want to scale up for something like an engine, but scale down for a flower or butterfly.

■ The scaled grid of squares enables you to transfer the sketch bit by bit by simply copying a single graph-paper square's worth of outline at a time on to the wall. It will help to number or letter the squares down and across on both the graph paper and the wall.

■ Transfer the sketch to the wall using a soft-leaded pencil, chalk or charcoal, all of which can be rubbed out if you make a mistake, and obliterated once

**4** Paint the mural in and obliterate any grid lines. As you gain confidence you may draw directly on the wall.

the painting is finished (although charcoal can smudge).

■ Once the whole sketch has been transferred to the wall, you can paint it. Decide in advance, on the graph-paper sketch, which colors to use for each part of the picture, and then use one color at a time – rather like painting by numbers. You will need several different-sized brushes: decorating brushes for large areas of paint, and artists' paintbrushes for detail and for smaller areas.

You need to be quite an experienced artist to make a mural completely realistic. For beginners, it is safer, and will look better, to paint a mural for children with flat, clear colors rather than trying to make it look like a "proper" painting, with too many tints, colors and details. But highlighting certain areas with a little off-white is worth doing if you are confident.

To protect a water-based painting, coat it with clear matte polyurethane varnish once it has dried. This also enables you to wipe dirty marks off the wall.

# Painting woodwork

The basic woodwork in a room normally includes the window frames, door and door frames (including those of built-in cupboards), and possibly baseboards. It may include extra items such as panelling, shutters or boxes built over pipes. The total amount of woodwork can add up to quite a large surface area, and its treatment will very much affect the look of the room.

If the wood has been stripped back to its natural state, you have a choice between painting, staining or clear varnishing. Simply waxing natural wood is not recommended: the wax sinks into the wood, making it difficult for the wood to accept future surface treatment, and gradually builds up a rather dull surface; wax is also too soft to protect the wood well.

Your choice of treatment will partly depend on the quality and condition of exposed wood. If it is attractive, with a good grain, simply wash it and rub it down (water raises the grain slightly to make this easier) and, when dry, coat it with clear polyurethane varnish or an acid catalyst sealer (which comes in two parts, that are mixed together to create an extremely durable finish). A woodstain often doubles as a protective sealing coat but will be much harder to remove, so be quite sure you have chosen a color you like. Woodstains now come in a wide variety of shades, some not at all wood-colored, and you can even mix your own. Several are water based, which makes them easier to remove. Some colored varnishes, where the color is carried in the transparent varnish coat, are only too easy to remove!

Oil-based gloss paint is a very effective cover for wood: protective, attractive and easy to clean. You can buy a non-drip or "jelly" gloss paint which is less glossy than the more free-flowing (or "alkyd") kinds, but which is quick drying, and very tough and resistant to impact. Gloss colors can be chosen from manufacturers' more special shades in the same way as latex, though many people prefer to stick to white for woodwork, which goes well in any room scheme.

If you are painting or stencilling a floor, you could use acrylic paint, floor paint (for a solid, opaque look), stencil crayon or wood dyes or stains. These are runny, so use a dry brush, wipe off the excess carefully and, if they are just too liquid, thicken by adding a little clear matte varnish.

## Preparing wood

Preparation for painting the woodwork in a room is important. (For filling and making good, see page 101.) Stick masking tape along the windowpanes next to the wood to be painted and wide sticky tape down along the edges of the carpet that cannot be moved. Have a bottle of turpentine and clean rags at the ready to wipe any spills – oil-based paint is hard to remove.

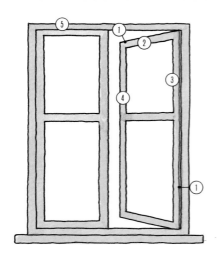

When painting a window frame, paint the edges in contact with the outer frame first then follow the order shown. Paint windows early in the morning.

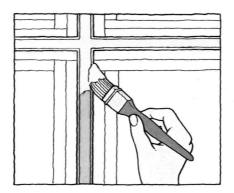

Before painting, cover the edges of the glass with masking tape to keep it clean. Use a cutting-in brush for the glazing bars and a 25mm (1in) brush for the rest.

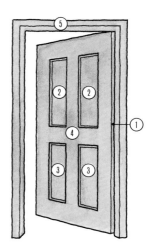

Paint a panelled door in the order indicated. Paint a flat door frame and the door edge first, then whole door from the top down, working from the hinge side.

Always paint wood with the grain: follow the way the visible grain runs, whether using paint or varnish. Do not overload your brush or you will create drips.

Bare wood will need a primer, either leadless wood or an all-purpose primer, but not an undercoat. A previous layer of paint, rubbed down, will not need a primer (except on bare patches) but will need an undercoat, especially if the color is going to be changed. Dirt and wax on natural wood can be removed with four parts of turpentine to one part linseed oil. French polish can be removed with a denatured alcohol. To clean painted wood, use detergent and warm water.

If you are stencilling a painted floor or piece of furniture, you need to "key" the areas where the stencil will go by lightly sanding them with very fine steel wool or fine sandpaper. If you have just repainted a floor, allow it to dry for at least a week before stencilling, in case moisture evaporating from the paint later causes the stencil to lift. Protect the areas you do not want touched by paint by taping newspaper over with masking tape.

## Painting procedure

Paint the woodwork after using latex paint on the walls but before putting on wallpaper. The brushes and pads used for painting narrow areas of woodwork, such as glazing bars, will be about 1in (25mm). For door panels and

baseboards, you can use a wider one, 2in (50mm).

Allow the first coat of paint to dry, and then rub down with fine grade abrasive paper or steel wool to remove any tiny paint bumps, perhaps around dust particles. Wipe off the surface thoroughly, then apply the second coat.

## Stencilling on wood

In a children's room stencils could be used to cheer up plain cupboard fronts, decorate a toy box or bring interest to a plain wooden floor. Natural wood, or wood painted with a water- or oil-based eggshell paint, or with a matte varnish, should take stencilling well. Even irregular-surfaced wooden floors can be stencilled on, provided the surface is prepared first (see above). Always use a non-toxic paint in a child's room; some fast-drying stencil paints will be unsuitable. Choose colors that are not too bright and garish for stencilled furniture.

If you are stencilling a flat surface, such as a cupboard door, a single central motif will look good. A wooden toy box could be stencilled along its front or lid, a chair along the back top rail. On a floor, you could restrain yourself to a swag or other motif at each corner, or make a stencil border,

or create an all-over pattern, either regular or random. Flowers, stars, animals or clowns are possible themes which could be sprinkled about or used as a border. Or the stencil can be based on purely abstract or geometric shapes, which will be easier to do. *Method* First, clean the floor or piece of furniture to remove old dirt, polish or wax (see above).

You will need to find the center of a floor in order to position a pattern or border. Stretch string diagonally between opposite corners of the room, fixing it with a drawing pin: where the two lengths of string cross will be the room's center. Mark the stencil positions with chalk. For a border around the room, measure the required distance out from the wall; measure diagonally from the corners.

The basic stencilling method is the same as for walls (see pages 106-107). Once the stencilling is finished and dry, protect it with three layers of clear, semi-matte varnish. Sand lightly and brush the dust away in between coats.

*A simple stencil border and all-over pattern add interest to these varnished floorboards and brighten up a very practical choice.*

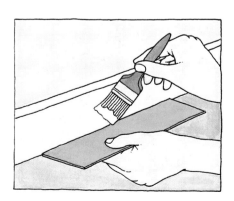

Hold a piece of card or plastic shield under baseboards, to prevent drips on to the floor. Use it on the top edge of baseboards, as a shield.

# Wallpapering

The walls to be papered should be clean, dry and as flat as possible – see page 98. If the base layer is just one layer of completely sound, well stuck-down printed wallpaper (i.e. not embossed relief or with a plastic surface), you can paper on top of this. But if it is at all loose or in poor condition, do not paper on top: the new wallpaper will simply pull the old away together with it. If the base layer is new plaster, you must wait at least six months to let the wall dry out before wallpapering.

On unpainted plaster, new or old, paint first with dilute latex, or size, using either glue size or thinned-down wallpaper paste. This prevents the plaster absorbing water from the wallpaper paste, and the slightly slippery surface of the dry size or paste will make it easier to position sheets of wallpaper when hanging. If you intend to hang a ready-pasted vinyl paper, use adhesive containing fungicide as size.

Always complete the painting of walls and woodwork in a room before you hang paper.

## Equipment

A folding pasting table is essential for wallpapering – besides being quite cheap, it is the right width, very light and easy to store. A 4in (100mm) paintbrush makes a perfectly good paste-applying brush.

If you plan to hang ready-pasted wallpaper, you can do without the pasting brush, and the table becomes optional, though you will still find it useful for cutting, matching patterns and marking lengths of paper. But you will need a trough for soaking the wallpaper – these are often sold with the ready-pasted paper.

## Measuring and cutting

Before you start measuring, mix the paste according to the manufacturer's instructions, leaving it to thicken in the bucket. It is a good idea to tie a piece of string across the bucket to use to scrape paste off the brush.

Wallpaper patterns are now designed to butt at the edge of strips, and, provided the pattern is relatively small, you can start hanging in one of

several places. If you start near a corner of the main window wall, this will give you a chance to get your hand in by hanging a few lengths on a plain wall with no awkward features. Then paper along the side walls, working away from the light. Some people prefer starting with the strips either side of the window. But do not start the actual papering in a corner, thinking to line the paper up with the wall edge. You cannot rely on it being true, and the same goes for door and window frames. The only straight line to trust is the plumbline.

If your paper has a bold pattern, however, you should center the first strip above or down any major room feature such as a chimney breast or a main window. If you don't, the eye may be drawn to an awkward join.

Having chosen your starting point, measure out from the top corner a distance about 1in (25mm) less than the width of the paper. Repeat the measuring at intervals down the walls, marking the spot each time with a pencil, then join up the marks by using

## EQUIPMENT

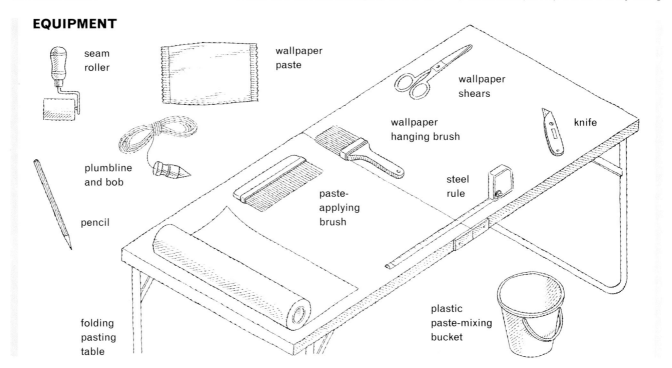

seam roller

wallpaper paste

plumbline and bob

pencil

wallpaper shears

wallpaper hanging brush

knife

paste-applying brush

steel rule

folding pasting table

plastic paste-mixing bucket

a plumbline. Chalk it first then snap it against the wall. A self-chalking one makes this easier. You will find it useful to have a helper to steady the plumb-bob once it has settled. This vertical line is a guide to measure the height of the wall for the whole room. If you suspect that the wall heights are very uneven, repeat the measurement in other places.

Unroll the wallpaper on to the table and measure out the drop, plus about 4in (100mm), using a steel rule. If the wallpaper has a feature pattern, choose a good starting place for the top of the drop. Do not start in the middle of a Superman's nose, for example, but make sure Superman's head is at the top of the wall – not all in the margin which will be trimmed off. Cut the drop, using wallpaper shears. Write "top" on the back of the paper at what will be the top end.

You can now use this length to measure out the next drops, matching patterns up as you go. It is easier and more economical of paper if you keep two or three rolls on the go, measuring out the pattern match from whichever will do it with least wastage. Write "top" on the back of each one. Watch out for papers with instructions to "reverse alternate lengths." You must remember to reverse the roll: every other drop is hung upside down.

### Pasting

Once you have cut a few drops of wallpaper, paste a small batch. Experienced wallpaperers try to develop a rhythm of working: cut several drops, paste a few drops, then either hang the first drops or cut more while the paste soaks into the first ones (but never allow it to over-soak), then hang the first ones and paste the next batch. Take it slowly at the beginning though: pasted wallpaper tears easily, and you want to concentrate your efforts on putting it on the wall smoothly and correctly.

To paste paper, spread it face down on the clean dry table. Dip the pasting

brush into the paste and draw it over the stretched string to wipe off excess paste. You must not get any paste on the table: it will spoil the surface of the paper. Paste by starting in the center of one end, then pull the paper gently to overlap the edges of the table so that you paste only it, not the table, brushing away from the center and only in the away direction. If you bring the paste-covered brush back still on the paper, there is a risk that it will smear paste under the edge of the wallpaper and on to its face.

### MEASURING AND PASTING

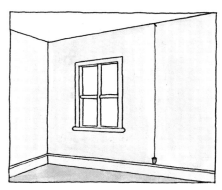

**1** Measure the height at the ends and center of the wall and add 4in (100mm) to the greatest figure to give the drop. Measure out this length of paper.

**2** Measure out the next drops, matching the pattern (cut off waste from the top). Cut enough lengths for all of one wall at once.

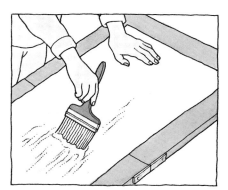

**3** Brush the paste on first down the middle of a table-length section of paper, then on the edge furthest away from you and finally the nearest edge.

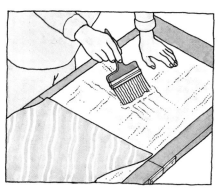

**4** Fold over the pasted end to the middle, pasted sides inwards, then shift the paper along the work surface and paste the rest of the length.

First paste the top half of the paper, then loosely fold this half over, with paste sides together, and move the paper along to paste the bottom half of the drop. Then fold the bottom edge of the paper up towards the other folded edge. If the drop is long, fold the paper in sections as you paste, like a concertina, so that no pasted side ever touches the face and so that the folded drop can easily be carried over your arm. Drape each pasted length over a stand or chair back as it is folded. Paste a small batch at a time.

# Hanging wallpaper

To hang the first strip of wallpaper, carry the pasted drop over your arm, top uppermost, and offer it up to the top of the wall where you have drawn the line. Leaving a trimming margin of about 2in (50mm) overlapping the top of the wall, align the edge of the drop with the line chalked on the wall. Use the open palms of your hands to maneuver the paper, to reduce the risk of tearing. Open out the top half of the drop and use the paper hanging brush to gently but firmly smooth it down, working from the top downwards, and from the middle out to the edges. Ease out any air bubbles as you work. When you are halfway down, let the rest of the paper go and smooth this down on to the wall. There should be an overlapping margin at the bottom of the wall as well as the top if you have measured correctly.

Once you are satisfied with the fit

*This bold children's wallpaper is thrown into relief by the use of a matching frieze and plainer pattern.*

and stick of the paper, trim off the margins. Use the back of the shears to push the paper into the angle between wall and ceiling, running them along to make a crease. Peel the paper away from the wall just enough to expose this crease and carefully trim off the excess. Refit the paper back in place and repeat where the bottom of the drop overlaps the baseboard. Fold up and throw away the sticky offcuts before you tread on them.

Hang the next drops in the same way, using the edge of the last drop as the vertical to push each one up against. Run a seam roller down the joins of flat wallpaper to ensure that the edges are stuck firmly to the wall. Use the bristles of the hanging brush on embossed or relief wall coverings instead of a seam roller.

### Hanging paper around fixtures
*Corners* Since room corners are rarely true verticals, you should paper a corner with two pieces. Measure from the last piece to the corner angle several times down the wall. For an

## PAPER-HANGING

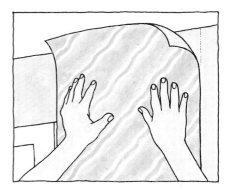

**1** Take the pasted drop over your arm and hold the top against the wall, using the flat palms of your hands.

**2** Unfold the bottom half and brush the paper on to the wall from the center outward to remove any air.

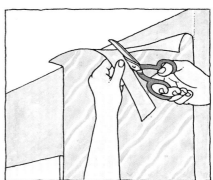

**3** Push the paper into the angle of wall and ceiling, running the side of your shears along to define the crease. Pull the paper away, trim off excess, and re-stick.

inward corner, add ½-⅝in (10-15mm) to the widest measurement you get, and measure this on to the back of the wallpaper from the matching edge. Then cut the drop to this width, as straight as possible, and hang in the usual way, brushing the overlap firmly into the corner. Then hang the strip you had cut off to a plumbline drawn parallel to the corner on the adjacent wall. If the corner is vertical, you will be able to butt-join this piece to the corner overlap of the other piece; otherwise overlap the second piece.

Use the same method for an external corner, overlapping the first piece over the corner and hanging the second to slightly overlap the turned edge.

*Doors* To hang around a door, hang the drop as usual when you reach the door. Part of it will cover the door frame. Brush the paper gently to the edge of the frame and you will see where the corner of the projecting door frame comes. Make an angled cut (at 45°) from the edge of the paper up to the door frame corner, which will free the paper above and to the side of the door. Brush it into the angles and trim, hanging the top part over the door frame. Then hang a short section above the door before hanging the next long drop on the other side.

*Windows* To hang around a flush window in a frame, do the same as for a door, but making a second freeing cut downwards at an angle to enable the paper to tuck into the bottom corner of the frame and in order to paper under as well as over the window frame. Cut two short pieces, one for above and one for below the window, before hanging another long drop which will need freeing cuts to finish off the window.

If the window is in a reveal, hang the length of paper so it obscures one side of the window and reveal. Then, after marking the ceiling and baseboard trim lines, make straight cuts with the sharp shears parallel with the top and bottom of the reveal. Tuck the freed paper into the side of the reveal. If it doesn't quite reach the edge, cut a fillet of the right width to do so. Trim the paper off flush with the top of the reveal. Hang short pieces above and below, and then another long length for the other side of the reveal.

*Light switches* Light switches can be dealt with by turning off electricity, papering over the fitting, then making cuts at angles from the center of the fitting to create four triangular flaps of paper which can be trimmed off to tuck in behind the unscrewed fitting cover.

Or else you can simply trim the paper flush up to the light fitting itself.

*Radiators* To deal with a radiator without removing it, paper with an ordinary length, letting it fall over the radiator. Make a vertical slit where it arrives at the pipe, then drop the paper down behind the radiator, smoothing it down with a long-handled implement.

### Relief, vinyl and lining papers
Wallpapers with ready-pasted backs need soaking for the recommended length of time to activate the paste. This can be done while still in the trough. If the paste dries out, you will need a small bucket of conventional paste at the ready. Where vinyl paper overlaps vinyl, as at corners, you must use a special vinyl overlap adhesive.

Some papers, made from foamed polyethylene, require the adhesive to be put directly on the wall. Some are so light that the whole roll can be presented to the wall, sticking as you go down and then trimming off.

Hang lining paper in the same way as other wallpaper if the wall is to be painted, but lay it horizontally if it is to be used as backing for a wall covering. This will mean pasting longer strips, but they should be manageable if they are concertina-folded as pasted.

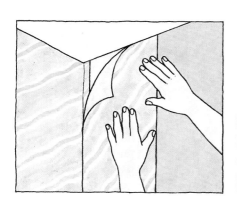

Dealing with corners: cut and fit a strip of paper wide enough to turn the corner by ⅝in (15mm). Hang the remaining offcut from this strip in line with a plumbline.

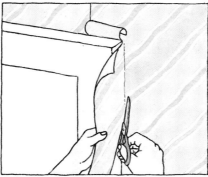

Window frames: let the length of paper drop over the frame, then lift it gently, and where the corner of the frame projects, make a cut at 45°. Trim off the surplus.

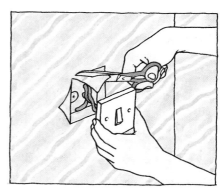

Light switches: turn off electricity at the electric box, paper over the fitting, then cut across the center of the switch. Unscrew switch plate to trim off excess.

# FURNISHINGS
# AND FITTINGS

To be able to put flesh on the bare bones of a room yourself, in the shape of curtains, blinds, cushions, quilts and shelves, is a useful skill. It frees you from the restrictions of shop-bought items, which may in any case cost more than you can afford, or which may not fit into a particular space. Shelf storage is essential for a child's books, toys and games, and if you can install shelves up to the ceiling in an alcove, you will be able to fit much more into the room than if you were limited to a small ready-made bookcase. Soft furnishings are equally important to add color, pattern, softness and warmth to any child's room, and it is not difficult to make up curtains yourself.

# Shelving/1

## TYPES OF SHELF SUPPORT

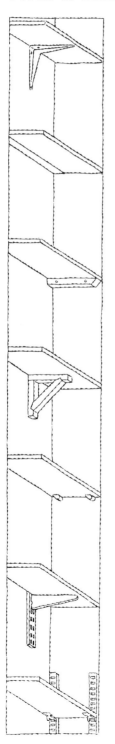

**Fixed shelving**

Steel angle bracket (for any position)

Cantilever shelving (only for light loads but any position)

Wooden battens (suitable for alcoves only)

Gallows bracket (suitable for any position)

**Adjustable shelving**

Grooved shelves supported on studs (for light loads in alcoves)

Metal back uprights with movable brackets (for any position)

Metal side uprights with movable support clips (for alcoves)

*A very versatile storage system has been built here to house books and other objects of different sizes as well as a comfortable working area. In a small room, such a system is an attractive feature as well as being practical.*

Though you can buy free-standing bookcases and shelf units, they won't necessarily fit a particular alcove or reach up to the ceiling. It is economical of space to put up your own shelves, which you can paint or stain to match an interior. And once you have learned the basic techniques you can adapt them to put up a single shelf in a useful but unusual position, such as the length of a wall above a door, to convert a wardrobe into shelf space, or to make drawer dividers and handy individual storage units.

You can make your own shelving, or buy ready-made adjustable components. Most suppliers will cut shelves to size for you. You will need certain basic tools, which you can probably borrow, but which are always a good household investment.

It is essential to understand the principles of installing into different types of wall, and to use the right kind of shelving and supports for the weight the shelves will have to bear. The best wall to attach shelves to is a solid one

(i.e. plaster on brick), because this is a firm substance into which to insert holding screws, and because a strong wall is the best for load bearing. The wall has to support not just the weight of the shelves themselves, which can be surprisingly heavy, but also their load. Books especially weigh a lot. If your fixing or shelf strength is too flimsy, the shelves will collapse – and it might be on top of a child.

The different kinds of shelf support are shown, left, and the types of wall plugs and screws are illustrated on the following pages.

You have to decide whether to use a ready-made shelving system or to make your own supports – this is easy for novices only in an alcove. Shop around first to inspect the types, finishes and prices of the different systems: you will find a wide variety. Bear in mind that you can paint cheaper metal brackets with special metal paint or with a metal primer first and then with gloss paint.

## Toolbox

You will need: a back saw, an electric saw if possible, a craft knife or pencil for cut guidelines; a large, medium and small screwdriver, plus one for Phillips screws; a hammer; a two-speed electric drill with two sets of twist bits (one set for spares) plus a masonry bit; a retractable steel tape; a carpenter's level (a butcher's level will do for horizontals and verticals, and to mark straight edges too); a try-square or, better still, a combination square, for making and checking right angles; a wood plane.

## Shelving materials

*Natural timber:* Very versatile, attractive and strong, but not cheap. It is prone to warp unless well seasoned.

Can be cut to size according to your requirements at a lumber yard.
*Medium density fiberboard:* Constructed of wood pulp and glue, this is very strong and quite cheap. It is sold in large sheets but is easy to work with. Medium density fiberboard needs only painting to look good.
*Particle board:* This is not an especially strong material, but it will do quite well for shelves which don't have to bear a lot of weight. It is most suitable if faced with a real wood or plastic veneer, which will both strengthen it and protect it against moisture, which otherwise weakens particle board. When boards are cut, the outer edges should be veneered too, with edging strip or wood edgebanding. Otherwise it can be sealed and painted. Particle board comes plain in large sheets, but is also available faced with a veneer, in a variety of shelf widths.
*Blockboard:* Consists of softwood battens sandwiched between layers of veneer. Comes in large sheets which you may be able to have cut to size.

When using, make sure the interior battens run the length of a shelf rather than the width. You can add edgebanding to smarten the shelves.
*Plywood:* Layers of thin veneer glued together to prevent warping. Can be faced with a final veneer of an attractive wood. Strong, quite expensive, and usually sold in large sheets. Can be difficult to cut without splintering, but better-quality plywood is less of a problem. You can always add edgebanding or strips of veneer to the edges of plywood shelves.

It is always worth asking your lumber yard or large do-it-yourself store if they offer a cut-to-size service for particle board, blockboard, plywood and medium density fiberboard, which are otherwise delivered in large sheets. But check the cost of this service: it can be expensive.

In terms of cost, particle board is the cheapest shelving material, followed in ascending order by sheathing quality plywood, medium density fiberboard, blockboard, good quality plywood and natural timber.

## TOOLBOX

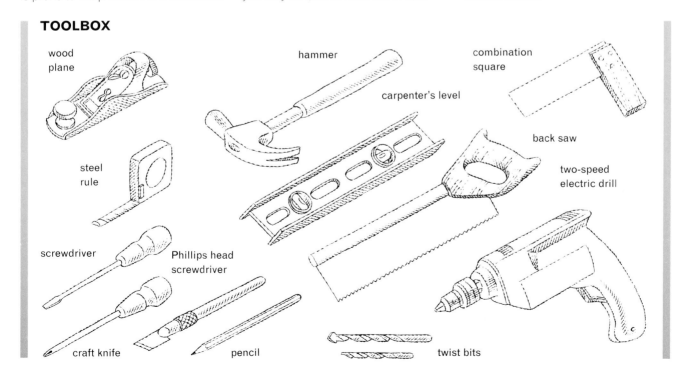

wood plane

hammer

combination square

carpenter's level

back saw

steel rule

two-speed electric drill

screwdriver

Phillips head screwdriver

craft knife

pencil

twist bits

# Shelving/2

## Wall-mounted shelves

It is possible to attach shelves to most walls, provided the load is spread across a number of supports and the correct wall fasteners are used (see below). But check first of all what your wall is made of.

Exterior walls are often constructed of brick, sometimes solid, sometimes with an air space or cavity between two layers. They may also be of concrete block. Interior walls may be solid brick, blocks or stud partitions composed of gypsum board (or, in some older homes, lath and plaster) hung on a wooden framework. Identify the material by tapping the wall: a solid wall gives a dead sound when knocked, and gypsum board gives a hollow sound, except for its wooden framework which gives a duller thud.

Shelves can be hung anywhere on solid walls, but watch out for electric cables and water pipes. Do not drill directly above, below or next to a plumbing or electrical fitting such as a light switch or electric outlet, or anywhere you suspect live wires may

run. If you can, check the wall first with an electronic detector which will show the presence of live wires. Standard or heavy-duty anchors can be used to hold screws on solid walls; use expanding anchors for heavy loads. Walls of hollow bricks or blocks will need cavity fixing devices of the collapsible anchor type, or concrete-block plugs.

On gypsum board, or lath and plaster, the shelf supports should be hung on the wooden framework. But if the shelves are to carry nothing heavy, and will not be heavy in themselves, you can use collapsible anchors or spring toggles which spread themselves against the back of the gypsum board and so stop the screw pulling out.

## Installing an adjustable shelving system

■ Place the left-hand upright wall bar where you wish it to hang on the wall. Push the screwdriver through the top screw hole and let the bar hang straight. The screwdriver will make a

slight positional mark on the wall.
■ Drill at this point, using the correct size of bit; use a depth guide bolt on the bit, or mark the bit with tape, to ensure you drill to the correct depth. Use an electric drill with a circuit breaker for safety, and never change a bit unless the machine is unplugged.
■ Insert the plastic anchor or other screw-holding device, then push a screw through the top hole in the wall bar and loosely screw it into the wall.
■ Ensure that the wall bar is hanging in a true vertical by holding a vertical carpenter's level or plumb-bob on or immediately next to it, adjusting it until correct. Then mark through all the screw holes with a sharp pencil – you may find this easier to do if someone is on hand to help you.
■ Drill holes, insert anchors, then attach the bar with the screws, tightening it securely. The top two screws in each upright are the most important, as these take most of the pulling load.
■ If you have a long carpenter's level or combination square, use this

## WALL FASTENINGS

*Raised-head screws are countersunk to attach architectural ware (e.g. handles).*

*Round-headed screws are used to secure flat metalwork, such as metal brackets or wall bars.*

*Flat-headed countersunk screws for general woodwork, which screw in flush or slightly below the wood surface.*

*Phillips screws need a Phillips head screwdriver. Particle board screws are ribbed all along. Dome-headed screws attach items such as mirrors. Screw covers and screw caps push or snap on.*

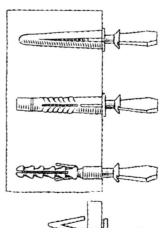

*General-purpose plain plastic anchor, for use in brick, high density blocks and concrete.*

*Heavy-duty plastic anchor. Ribbed for resistance to pulling out, good in loose material.*

*Finned concrete block anchor for concrete or concrete-block walls. Can be hammered in.*

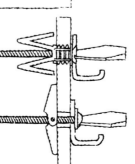

*Gypsum board plugs can be collapsible, or barbed, to spread the load in a different way.*

*Spring toggles are best for lath and plaster. The bolt of the toggle is fed through the fitting first.*

## ADJUSTABLE SHELVING

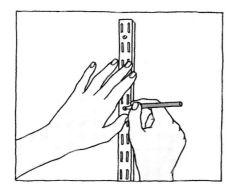

**1** Fix metal bars vertically on the wall by drilling at the pencil marks, inserting anchors and tightly screwing the bars down.

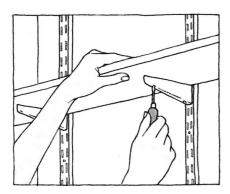

**2** The more uprights used, the better the load will be spread. Ensure that the distances between shelves are what you need, before positioning them.

horizontally to check the position of the next vertical. Slot a bracket into place. If you are only using two uprights, check the required distance for the next upright with one of the shelves you are going to use. If you are using several uprights, they should be an equal distance apart, spaced along the length of the shelf. Check distances with the rule, and attach each upright as you did the first.
■ When all the uprights are attached, slot in the brackets, place the shelves

on them and secure them to the brackets. Always check that you have space for the tallest item you want to place on the shelves before you attach them in their final position.

### Installing alcove shelving
To make this yourself, you will need solid wooden battens to support the sides and back of each shelf.
■ Cut wooden battens 2in by 1in (5cm by 2.5cm). You will need three per shelf: a long one to run along the back wall, and two short ones which should be 2in (5cm) shorter than the width of the shelf. Chamfer the front of each side batten to make it less obtrusive when viewed from the front or side.
■ Very few alcove walls are true in their dimensions, so plan where you want each shelf to go and measure each one individually. Mark lightly with a pencil on the wall the position not of the shelf but just below it – the thickness of the shelf and half the batten will come in between – and measure each width separately. You will probably find that you have to trim each shelf length slightly differently. If it is by a small amount, shave a wooden shelf with a wood shaver, otherwise trim carefully with a saw. An electric saw can speed up the work.
■ Mark holes 2in (5cm) in from the ends, and then at 12in (30cm) intervals, along the center line of each batten. For side battens, mark two or three equally spaced hole positions. Drill screw holes at these points.
■ Hold the first back batten on the wall over the pencil mark, place a carpenter's level on top, and adjust until it is exactly straight. Then mark with a pencil through the pre-drilled holes. Remove the batten and drill into the wall as for adjustable shelves.
■ Put anchors in the holes and screw through the batten firmly into the wall. Push the first side batten up against this back batten and place a carpenter's level across them at an angle till the side batten is level. Mark and drill screw holes.

## ALCOVE SHELVING

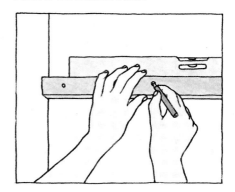

**1** Hold the pre-drilled batten on the wall, check with a carpenter's level and mark with a pencil through the screw holes. Drill the wall at the pencil marks.

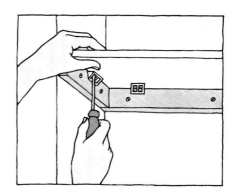

**2** A neat way to secure shelves is with plastic corner fastening blocks which screw into both shelf and battens. Align tops of blocks with tops of battens.

■ Repeat for the remaining battens.
■ You can then attach plastic corner fastening blocks to the middle of the side of each batten and a little way in from the ends of each rear batten, so that the tops of the blocks are level with the tops of the battens. Lay the shelf on the battens and screw up through the blocks. You may need to lift the shelf off to drill a little way into it where these corner block screws will sink into the underside. Or screw down through the shelf into the battens.

# Shelving/3

## METAL BRACKETS

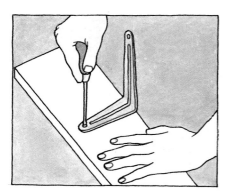

**1** Attach the shorter arm of the metal brackets to the underside of the shelves, 7-10in (18-25cm) from each end, spaced at 20-30in (50-80cm) intervals.

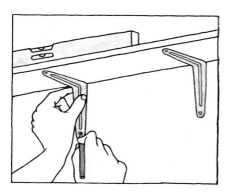

**2** Hold the shelf on the wall at the pre-marked position, using a carpenter's level. You may need help to mark the installing position through the holes.

## Installing shelving with metal brackets

Buy enough of the right size of metal support brackets for the width of shelf you want to install and the weight that the shelves will be supporting. Mark the positions of the shelves as for alcove shelving (see page 121).
■ If you are working on a solid wall, attach the brackets to the underside of the shelves. You will need a bracket about 7-10in (18-25cm) in from each end of the shelf, and the remaining

*This versatile cube unit can be adapted in size, and hung either way to suit the purpose.*

brackets should be spaced at 20-30in (50-80cm) intervals along the shelf, depending on the sturdiness of the shelf and the weight that it will be supporting. If the shelves are intended for something heavy, such as books, use more brackets. Screw the shorter arm of each bracket to the underside of each shelf.
■ Hold the shelf up on the wall at the pre-marked position, with a carpenter's level resting on top. You will need a helper to mark with a pencil the position of the attaching screws through the bracket holes of the longer wall arm, once the shelf is perfectly straight on the wall.
■ Repeat for the other shelves, then drill and plug the holes and screw the shelf brackets into position.
■ If you are working on a gypsum-board wall, the positions of the brackets should align with the hidden wooden uprights. If they will not satisfactorily do this, you will have to use the batten method (see page 121).

## Making a cube unit

This simple unit is basically a box with a back to make it stronger, divided into six compartments. The proportions given here can be scaled up or down to make a larger or smaller unit. It can be made from wood, medium density fiberboard, particle board or blockboard. While beginners might be tempted to ask a supplier to cut pieces to size from those materials which are normally delivered as large sheets, this will add quite a bit to the cost and might not make it worth the effort of constructing it yourself rather than buying a ready-made equivalent.

Instructions are given here for making the unit from ¾in (17.5mm) medium density fiberboard, though you could use ½in (12mm) thick MDF for a unit which will carry no heavy weight. Ideally you want a sheet measuring 3ft by 2ft (915mm by 610mm), though you may have to buy one bigger than this if they do not come any smaller. This plain material should be painted after construction, which will conceal nailheads and enable you to match other colors in the room. The cube unit can be hung horizontally or vertically.

From the sheet delivered, you need to cut out two pieces measuring 25½in by 6in by ¾in (634mm by 150mm by 17.5mm), one 24in by 6in by ¾in (600mm by 150mm by 17.5mm), four pieces 12in by 6in by ¾in (300mm by 150mm by 17.5mm). You will also need a piece of hardboard 25½in by 12in (635mm by 300mm) for the backing sheet, some 1½in (35mm) and 1in (25mm) nails, and some mirror plates for attaching the unit to the wall.

■ Make the basic frame by nailing the four edge pieces together. The horizontals should be placed inside and flush with the top edge of the verticals. Check that the angles form 90 degrees. As long as the components have been cut accurately, the backing board should fit on to the frame exactly, and can now be nailed to it with 1in (25mm) nails.

■ Cut two slots ¾in (17.5mm) wide at equal intervals in the remaining upright – i.e. the center point of each slot should be 8in (200mm) from each end of the sheet. They should extend for half the depth of the upright – 3in (75mm). Cut slots to match midway along the two horizontal shelves, again ¾in (17.5mm) wide and for half the depth of the shelves.

■ Slot the upright into the corresponding slots in the horizontal shelves and push and then gently hammer home. Fit this assembly into the frame and check that everything is properly squared up. Secure with 1in (25mm) nails from the back and with 1½in (35mm) nails through the top and sides. The adhesion of the outer frame and the inner assembly to the backing board can be strengthened with wood glue, if you like.

■ If you prefer rounded to sharp corners, you can chamfer the four outer corners of the frame by sanding them into a smooth curve.

■ Prime and gloss paint the unit in your chosen color. Attach mirror plates to the back, screwing them through the hardboard into the outer horizontal and/or vertical shelves.

*The most economical way of cutting a single sheet of particle board or medium density fiberboard is shown below.*

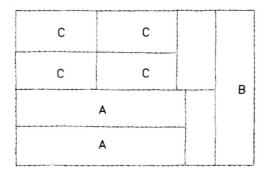

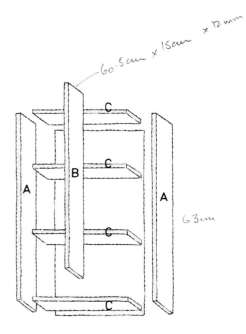

## MAKING THE CUBE UNIT

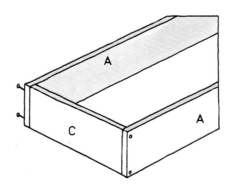

**1** Nail the four edge pieces together, with the shorter, horizontal lengths placed inside the verticals. Check that the angles of the outer frame are right angles.

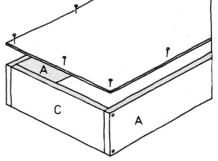

**2** Nail the hardboard backing sheet to the outer frame at the edges, using 1in (25mm) nails. It should fit exactly and will make the unit more rigid.

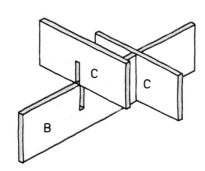

**3** Cut two slots in the remaining vertical lengths, and slots to match in the middle two horizontal shelves. Fit together, then assemble inside the frame.

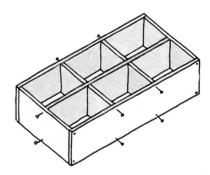

**4** Secure the cube unit with 1½in (35mm) nails through all joins. If the shelves are to house anything heavy, you may strengthen the joints with wood glue.

# Making curtains/1

Before you head for the shops to buy the chosen fabric for your child's room, you must decide on the style of curtains. The two factors which determine the amount of material you will need are: the type of heading you will use, and how far the curtains will fall – to the sill edge, the top of a radiator or the floor.

You will also have to decide whether the curtains are to be lined and/or interlined, how they will be hung – from a track or a pole – and whether they will have a tie-back. Unless you are using a decorative pole, you might want to consider making a cornice, to finish off the top neatly.

Most assistants are very practiced at calculating the amount of fabric needed, provided they are supplied with the dimensions of the windows. Never buy fabric without taking these measurements with you.

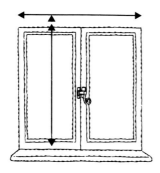

To calculate the amount of curtain fabric, first measure down from the track or pole position above the window to where the curtains will end. The width to measure is that of the pole or track, not the window.

## Measuring

An extending steel tape is more reliable than a fabric one. Either fix the track or pole in position, or mark where it will go on the wall (ideally 6in/15cm from the top of the window), then measure down from this point to where the curtains will end. Add 8in (20cm) for hem and heading. This will give you the "drop:" the length of each width that you will need.

The total fabric width is not the width of the window but the amount of material needed to provide the finished effect when it is gathered up on a curtain heading. Different headings require different amounts of fabric (see Types of Heading, right). Since curtain material generally comes in rolls 48in (120cm) wide, you often have to sew lengths or part-lengths together to achieve the right width of fabric for each curtain.

To calculate the amount of fabric you need, multiply the length of the curtain track or pole by the number required for your choice of heading (see right). Remember that you may want the track or pole to extend about 6in (15cm) beyond the window on each side in order to provide a space into which the curtains can be fully pulled back, to let more light in during the day. Divide this figure by the width (i.e. generally by 48in/120cm) of the fabric, and round up to the nearest whole number to obtain the number of fabric widths required per window, or pair of curtains. Then multiply the curtain length by the number of fabric widths you have calculated to give you the total length of fabric you need to buy.

Unless a washable fabric has been preshrunk, allow around three to four per cent extra for shrinkage. If you are buying a patterned fabric, remember to allow enough extra to match the pattern when joining lengths together. It is always better to be slightly generous in your calculation from the point of view of how the curtains will look – satisfyingly billowy rather than skimpily stretched.

## TYPES OF HEADING

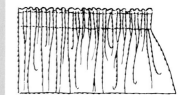

**Standard** Produces simple, even gathers. Especially suitable for lightweight or small, unlined curtains. Requires 1½-2 times the track length.

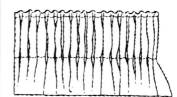

**Pencil pleat** Produces deep gathers and a more formal look. Tape depth varies from 1½-6in (4-15cm). Requires 2¼-2½ times the track length.

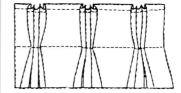

**Triple pleat (or pinch pleat)** Gathers curtains into clusters of three, spaced about 4in (10cm) apart. Tape depth 4-14cm (1½-5½in). Requires 2 times the track length.

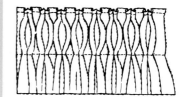

**Decorative** More unusual types give decorative headings such as smocking. Suitable for lightweight curtains. Requires 2 times the track length.

## Headings

These strips of strong fabric, bought by length, have pockets and an integral drawstring running through them. They perform the double function of attaching the curtain to the track or pole and giving the curtain a particular kind of gather and hang when the drawstring is pulled up. They are sewn to the top of the curtain and hooks are pushed through the pockets in the heading tape, then hooked on to the runners of a track or the rings of a pole to suspend the curtain. Deep headings make for a crisper look, and they offer the choice of two rows of pockets. If you put the hooks into the lower row, the curtains sit above the track and cover or partly cover it when the curtains are drawn; hooks in the top row allow curtains to hang from rings and reveal the pole. Some headings require special hooks. There are different weights of headings too: use lightweight kinds for sheer and thin curtains; if you need to gain stiffness, use iron-on interfacing. The main kinds of heading, and the fabric widths they require, are shown left.

## Cornices

A cornice looks a little like the top of an old-fashioned sentry box or the frill at the top of a Punch and Judy puppet theater. It disguises the actual top of the window and the track, giving a neat box edge to the windows. Cornices can be straight or decoratively edged; while a straight-edged cornice is potentially formal, it would be less so if covered with a cheerful material, and a decoratively-edged cornice could be used to make a very attractive feature in a child's room.

Most cornices consist of a top fabric and lining glued and stitched to a stiffener, such as buckram, then fixed on to a support board positioned just above the window. It can be fixed on either with decoratively headed tacks or with ordinary ones which can then be disguised by braid to form an edging to the cornice.

*The cornice board* can be made from plywood or medium density fiberboard. It normally projects 4in (10cm) from the wall and is cut from ⅝-¾in (1.5-2cm) thick ply or MDF. Its length should be slightly wider – 2in (5cm) either side – than the width of the window, and you should locate it 2-3in (5-8cm) above the top of the track. Fix the shelf, or board, to the wall with small angle brackets spaced at 12-16in (30-40cm) intervals across the width.

Nail a 4in (10cm) square of ply or MDF to each end. If the cornice extends over a large window, it may need a frontage of hardboard to give the cornice itself some extra support.

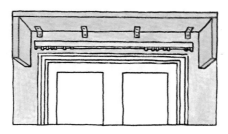

The cornice board is fixed to the wall just above the track, using small angle brackets. Nail a square-shaped piece of plywood or MDF to each end.

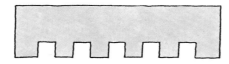

Cornices can be soft and gathered or stiffened with buckram cut into a variety of shapes. Decoratively shaped cornices lend themselves well to children's rooms.

The stiffened cornice material can be deeper than the depth between the shelf and the top of the window; how much deeper depends on the size of the window (a small window will look silly with a deep cornice) and the weight of the material you will use: cornices should not be too floppy.

## Making a fabric cornice

Calculate the amount of fabric needed, based on the width and depth of the cornice, allowing enough to cover the side panels. Center a complete fabric width, attaching panels at the sides if widths have to be joined. Remember to match a patterned material across the seams.

■ Cut the top fabric and lining to the correct size, allowing ⅝in (1.5cm) for turnings all around. The fabric stiffener should be cut to the exact size, without turning allowance.

■ Place the top fabric right side down, and position the stiffener centrally on it, leaving a turning all around.

■ Peel off the backing from the stiffener, then fold over the edges of the top fabric; clip the curves and press the turned edge in place.

■ Turn under and press the seam allowance of the lining and place over the stiffener, wrong sides together, matching the outer edges. Press firmly in place. Neatly slipstitch the lining to the turned edges of the top fabric.

■ Fold and crease the side-section turns, then fix the whole cornice to the cornice board, using double sticky-sided Velcro, adhesive or sticky pads.

The procedure for a decoratively edged cornice is the same, but you must obviously take more care in cutting the fabric out. Use a paper template cut in the desired outline to shape the edge. It is also possible to make a completely flat cornice, with a straight or shaped bottom edge, for windows recessed into a flat wall or with no bulky window frame. Make it from stiffened fabric as above, and stick it flat across suitable windows rather than on to a cornice board.

# Making curtains/2

### Unlined curtains

If possible, work on an empty table large enough to spread out the material (this is especially important if you have to make sure a one-way design is facing the right direction). To cut out the fabric widths, measure down and rule straight cutting lines across the fabric in tailor's chalk, then cut along them with sharp scissors. Remember to leave the allowance for seams and hems. To obtain half widths, fold a length of fabric, selvage to selvage, and cut along the fold with sharp scissors. Snip any selvages to release the tightly woven edge before hemming or stitching, otherwise the material will pucker.

■ Using a sewing machine, join the widths together for each separate curtain, with a seam allowance of ⅝in (1.5cm). So that these joining seams look smart and are strong, trim one edge of seam allowance in half, fold the wider seam allowance over the narrower and press it flat against the fabric. Then machine stitch down the seam again and press carefully.

■ Take double turnings of 1in (2.5cm) on the side edges, and a 3in (8cm) double hem on the bottom edge, pressing each layer to the wrong side. Miter (that is, fold in to form a neat, angled corner) the corners before stitching the turnings in place.

■ Slipstitch around the edges and the hem by hand, picking up just one or two threads of the fabric with each stitch so that the stitching is not too visible on the right side of the fabric. Enclose weights in the hem if needed to give a better hang to the curtains.

■ Measure up the finished length from the base of the curtain and mark it with a line of pins. Press over the top of the curtain at the pin line. The turnover should be concealed by the heading tape, so trim off any excess fabric before fixing the heading.

■ Attach the chosen heading across the top of each curtain, positioning it close to the top edge. Fold under about ½in (12mm) of tape at the ends.

Machine stitch in place, taking care not to stitch over the strings.

■ Pull up the tape to the required width and distribute the pleats evenly.

### Lined curtains

Linings can be loose or lock-stitched lightly to the curtain fabric across the whole curtain. Lock-stitching the lining is thought to be best for heavy materials or anything needing a highly professional finish. For a really good hang and high insulation, add interlining between the curtain and lining: the interlining needs to be lightly lock-stitched to the curtain fabric (see below).

You need the same amount of lining material as curtain fabric (less if you have allowed extra for a pattern match), but it should be about 1½in (4cm) narrower than the curtain fabric. It will need to be made up into curtain widths in the same way. But the seams of the lining and the curtain need only

be snipped into and pressed flat open.

■ Snip the selvages and raw edges of the seams every 4-6in (10-15cm) and press open. Then pin, tack and machine stitch the side edges of the lining to the curtain, with right sides together, using ⅝in (1.5cm) flat seams, to within 6in (15cm) of the hem. Clip the seams to prevent the fabric puckering.

■ Turn up a double hem of 1in (2.5cm) on the lining, miter the corners, and slipstitch to close the corners. Machine stitch along the hem.

■ Turn the lined curtain right side out, matching the centers of the lining and curtain. When you are confident that all is smooth and even, press the whole curtain, paying particular attention to the side edges.

■ Turn up a double hem of 5cm (2in), or deeper if you prefer, on the main fabric. Insert curtain weights if they are needed, and miter and finish as for unlined curtains.

*Floor-length curtains effectively frame a window during the day, especially when they are secured by pretty tie-backs. The roller blind intended to help keep out light during the day is linked to the curtains by its decorative border.*

## UNLINED CURTAINS

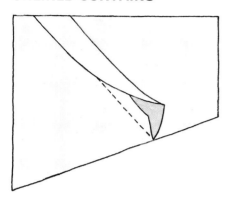

**1** Join together widths of fabric, trim one seam in half, fold over the other, press flat and stitch down.

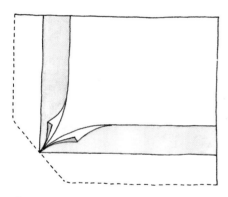

**2** To miter a corner, first fold in and press the corner of fabric, then cut off part of the corner to reduce bulk.

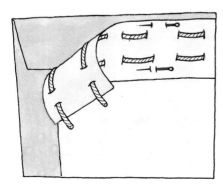

**3** Fold down the top edge of the curtain and pin on the heading tape, then baste and stitch it in place. Pull up the cords evenly to the required fullness.

■ Turn down the top edge, cutting and turning in the corners tidily, and add the heading tape.

### Lock-stitching a lining
Although this is a time-consuming procedure, the professional-looking results are worth the effort. By loosely stitching the lining to the fabric, the curtains hang better.
■ Make up the curtain widths, then fold a single hem of 2½in (6.5cm) along the side edges of the curtain fabric and lining, and a single hem of 6in (15cm) along the base, mitering the corners. Add curtain weights now if they are to be used.
■ Herringbone stitch around all these edges, taking just one or two threads of fabric. Because it involves sewing by hand, you should allow a fair amount of time for this stage.
■ Turn under ¾in (2cm) along the side edges of the lining and 2in (5cm) along the base, turning the corners in neatly. Trim off ¾in (2cm) from the top of the lining material.
■ Lay the curtain fabric on a flat surface, right side down, and spread the lining on top, right side up, ¾in (2cm) from the top. Match the centers and when all is smooth, pin down the middle all along the curtain's length.
■ Fold the lining back to expose the pins and at this junction use long loose lock-stitches, in a thread that matches the curtain fabric, to join the lining to curtain along its length. Make rows of stitching about 16in (40cm) apart.
■ Repeat this process across the whole width of the curtain, working out from the center in both directions, always starting at the top and working down towards the hem but stopping just short of it.
■ Slipstitch the lining to the curtain turnings along the side edges and hem.
■ Attach the curtain heading tape to the top edge with machine stitching.
■ If interlining is to be used as well, first lock-stitch this to the wrong side of the curtain fabric, then lock-stitch on the lining.

## LINED CURTAINS

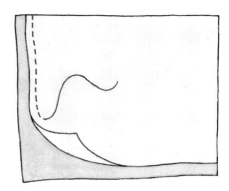

**1** With right sides together, lay the lining over the curtain fabric and stitch together at the sides; turn right side out.

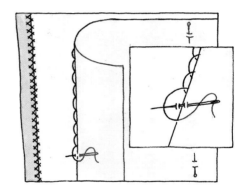

**2** To lock-stitch a lining, pin the lining in rows down the length of the fabric. Fold back the lining to the pins; lock-stitch.

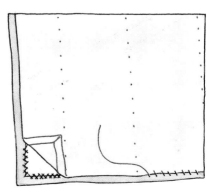

**3** Turn under the lining at the sides and base, mitering the corners, and press. Then slipstitch lining to curtain along the sides and hem.

# Making blinds/1

In terms of their operation, blinds fall into two groups: roller blinds, which roll up as the name implies, and Roman, Austrian and festoon blinds, all of which pull up by a series of cords and rings attached to the back of the blind. A very wide window will not take a blind satisfactorily, because a blind that is wider than it is long will not hang or roll very well.

Roller blind kits are widely available, and so are separately sold fabric stiffeners, as well as tapes and eyelets for Roman and Austrian blinds. So it is easier than you might think, and certainly cheaper, to make blinds yourself. Festoon blinds, being the most complicated, have been omitted from the practical instructions given on these pages.

Roller blinds fit well with curtains, and can be pulled down for a child's daytime nap or to cut out bright sunlight in the early mornings.

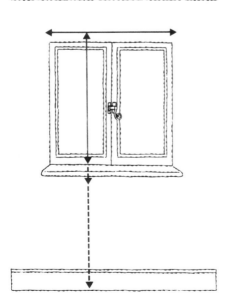

Measure for a blind from the top of the roller, batten or track and down to the bottom of the sill. The width of the track or batten determines the blind width.

## Measuring up

*Roller blinds* It is usual for roller blinds to hang inside the window recess where there is one. Where there is not, the blind is mounted on a suitable flat part of the window frame or on the wall immediately beyond the frame, in which case you should plan to hang the blind slightly wider than the window, to prevent any gaping. To obtain the width of roller required, measure from one side of the chosen position to the other, deducting ⅝in (1.5cm) at each side for the pin end and spring mechanism. The width of fabric is the same as that of the roller, except that ¾in (2cm) should be added to the total for side hems if you plan to stiffen your own fabric with a spray stiffener rather than using pre-stiffened fabric.

For the drop, measure from the top of the roller (which fits into a recess 1¼in/3cm from the top to allow for the full roll of blind to fit in) to the bottom of the window frame. Add an extra 12in (30cm) for the bottom hem casing and for enough extra material at the top to ensure that the roller is still covered with fabric even when fully extended: otherwise it will tend to look rather unsightly.

*Roman blinds* Roman blinds are suspended from a wooden batten, attached either to the window frame, to the wall above, or to the soffit of a recess. In a window recess, measure from the top of the batten to the sill. The width of the fabric is the same as the width of the batten, plus 1¼in (3cm) for side turnings. On a window with no recess, the batten is mounted on supports just above the window, and the length is still calculated from the batten position. The length of fabric should include 6in (15cm) for the hem casing and margin to attach to the batten. The face and sides of the blind batten can have fabric glued on to them, as they will be partly on view.

*Austrian blinds* These hang on a special track fitted with eyelets, which fits into a window recess or is attached

## TYPES OF BLINDS

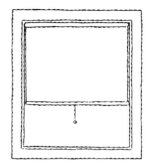

**Roller** Can be bought ready-made or home-made with a kit. Gives clean, simple lines and combines well with curtains.

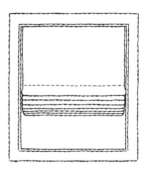

**Roman** Pulls up unfussily into even folds of fabric, giving a softer, more elegant effect than a roller blind.

**Austrian** A ruched blind, using a large amount of material. Lining and frill make it even fuller.

to the wall just above the window. Measure the drop from the top of the track and add on a third as much again. Calculate the width by doubling the track length. For a window without a recess, the track should extend 6in (15cm) beyond the edges of a plain window but be flush with the edges of a window frame.

## Making a roller blind

Buy a standard weight blind kit or a heavy-duty one for large windows. The kit usually comprises a roller with a spring mechanism, screws and supports, a lath to weigh down the base and a small pull cord to screw on to the lath. If you cannot find a size of roller the exact width of your window, buy the next largest and saw it to fit: a cap will be provided to cover the cut end. Attach the roller by screwing in the support brackets, 1¼in (3cm) below the top of a recess, and slotting in the roller. Mount the bracket for the square pin on the left-hand side of the window and the bracket for the round pin of the winding mechanism on the right. Use plastic anchors in drilled holes if you are attaching the brackets on a wall.

Fabric for roller blinds has to be specially stiffened first. Most department stores and specialist shops sell a good range of ready stiffened fabrics, as well as stiffening liquid or spray to enable furnishing cottons to be used for roller blinds. You will have to use closely woven, medium-weight cotton for best results.

■ Cut out the fabric, making sure the edges are square and the pattern repeats centered. Use a large T-square to help you cut the fabric absolutely on the square.

■ If you plan to spray-stiffen an ordinary furnishing fabric, turn a ⅜in (1cm) hem down the side edges and zigzag machine stitch over the raw edges. Then stiffen the fabric with the proprietary spray.

■ Make the casing by folding over a double 1½-2in (4-5cm) turning to the wrong side; press and stitch across

this and down one side to make a casing into which you can slide the lath. The lath should be cut ½in (12mm) shorter than the finished width of the blind. Stitch to close the casing.

■ Screw down the cord pull in the exact center of the lath, on either the wrong side or the right depending on its look and style. Remember to check that you can reach this pull when the blind is fully rolled up.

■ At the top edge, with the fabric right side up, fold over and press ⅝-¾in (1.5-2cm) of material in order to cover the roller to the marked guideline. If the roller does not have a guideline, draw one on with a pencil.

■ Attach with tacks at ¾in (2cm) intervals, making sure the fabric is firmly attached at each end. To make sure the winding mechanism is at the right tension, roll up the blind reasonably firmly by hand and insert it into the holding brackets. Pull down as far as the bottom of the window frame and release: it should spring back to the top, but not too wildly. Re-roll if the tension is wrong, either more loosely or more tightly.

## Making a Roman blind

Roman blinds pull up into a series of crisp, horizontal folds, by means of a cord threaded through rings. The rings are usually attached to tapes running vertically across the width of the blind at intervals. Alternatively, the rings or eyelets can be attached to narrow timber rods contained in pockets attached horizontally to the back of the blind. This gives the blind more rigidity. The method outlined below uses tapes. You can buy ringed tape but it is more common to find looped tape, on which you attach your own rings.

Roman blinds are made from lined material, which should be a good-quality fabric, such as glazed cotton. The lining should be the same length but 1¼in (3cm) narrower than the fabric. A Roman blind could be lined with blackout material to keep out light from a child's room in summer.

## MAKING A ROLLER BLIND

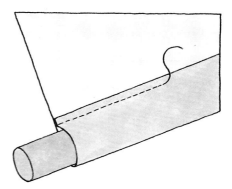

**1** Cut stiffened fabric as described and fold up a double 1½in (4cm) hem to the wrong side. Stitch to make lath casing.

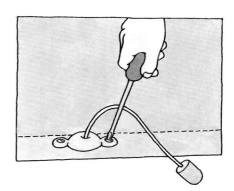

**2** Attach the cord pull firmly to the center of the bottom lath on right or wrong side of the blind.

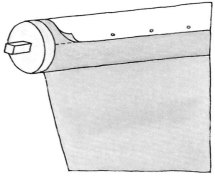

**3** Place top edge of blind along guideline on the roller, holding it with the spring mechanism to the left. Hammer in tacks at ¾in (2cm) intervals.

# Making blinds/2

Calculate the amount of ringed tapes and cord needed: the tapes will be the same length as the blind and are fixed between 10-12in (25-30cm) apart across the width of the blind. The amount of cord will be double the length of the finished blind plus the width, multiplied by the number of tapes needed. You also need a screw eye for each tape and a wooden lath for the bottom of the blind.

■ Join any widths of fabric with flat seams, with part-widths on the outside. Make up lining in same way.

■ With right sides and centers together, pin, tack and stitch the lining to the fabric at the sides, using ⅝in (1.5cm) seams. Snip into the seams, press open and turn to right side.

■ Pin the fabric centers together and press flat so that, on the back of the blind, the margins of the blind fabric can be seen on either side of the lining; they should be the same width.

■ Turn up the bottom edge of the whole blind ⅜in (1cm) then 4in (10cm) on the wrong side, to form a hem which will include the casing for the lath. Pin the hem in place.

■ Pin on the lengths of ringed tape at intervals between 10-12in (25-30cm) apart, down the full length of the blind, starting with the seam lines. All rings must line up horizontally across the blind, ending with the last ring ½in (1cm) from the hem edge. Tuck the ends of the tape into the pinned hem.

■ Using the sewing machine's zipper foot, stitch the tapes down both sides through all thicknesses. Stitch across the top of the hem, catching in the tape ends, and stitch a second row of horizontal stitching about 1½in (4cm) below this for the casing.

■ Insert the lath and slipstitch both side edges to hold it in position.

■ On the top edge, zigzag stitch the lining and fabric together, catching in the ends of the tapes. Fold ¾in (2cm) of blind over the top of the batten and attach it with tacks or staples on the wide side. Position screw eyes along the underside of the batten to correspond with the tops of each row of ringed tape.

■ Cut the cord into equal lengths, the same number as there are tapes. Starting at the right or left hand side, knot the cord to the bottom ring and thread it up through all the rings in that row. On reaching the top, thread the cord through all the screw eyes on the batten till you reach the far side. Repeat until the cords are hanging together at one side of the blind.

■ Replace the batten on the wall or window frame, attaching the blind to the window, and attach a cleat to the window frame on whichever side the bundle of cords lies.

■ Trim the cords to the same length and knot together, level with the sill. Raise the blind and wind the bunch of cords around the cleat. The cords can alternatively be threaded through a brass drop weight and tied.

## Making an Austrian blind

Austrian blinds operate in a similar way to Roman blinds but are constructed like a curtain, and hang from a special Austrian blind track or a pole. The most suitable heading tape is pencil pleat. Austrian blinds are often finished with a frill at the base.

■ Make up your fabric width twice the width of the track, lining it in the usual way. If you are making an unlined blind, fold a hem, single (1¼in/3cm) or double (⅜in/1cm) depending on the bulk of the fabric, along both sides of the blind and press, pin, baste and stitch in place.

*The uncluttered lines of a Roman blind suit the simplicity of this nursery. A striped fabric lends itself particularly well to this style of window treatment.*

## MAKING A ROMAN BLIND

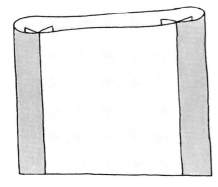

**1** The width of the blind is the batten length plus 3½in (9cm), the lining 1¼in (3cm) narrower. Join together.

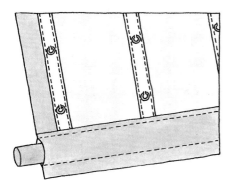

**2** Pin lengths of ringed tape to the lined side of the blind at 10-16in (25-40cm) intervals. Stitch down.

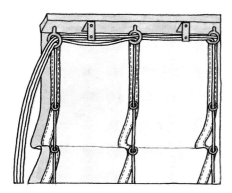

**3** Position screw eyes in the underside of the batten to correspond to the tapes. Thread each cord through its rings and through all screw eyes.

■ On the wrong side of the blind, pin, baste and stitch the outer two rows of ringed tape 4in (10cm) from the hemmed edges and 1¼in (3cm) up from the base edge. Attach the rest of the ringed tape at 12in (30cm) intervals, making sure that the rings lie in horizontal parallel lines across the fabric.

■ If you want a frill, cut a deep hem piece, about 6½in (16cm) wide, and twice the width of the blind fabric. Turn under a double ⅜in (1cm) hem around the sides and base of the frill strip, mitering the corners. Run gathering stitches through the top of the frill, and pull up, until the frill is the same width as the blind. If the frill is very long, gather it in sections. Then join them with a ¾in (2cm) seam, catching in the tape edges tidily. Snip the seam and press flat open; stitch to neaten.

■ If you don't want a frill, turn up a hem of ⅝in (1.5cm), then 1in (2.5cm).

■ Turn down the top edge of the blind by ⅜in (1cm). Attach the heading tape and pull it to the required width. Attach hooks to the gathered heading tape.

■ If you want to slide the blind on to a pole, omit the heading tape and turn over 5in (12.5cm) at the top of the blind, turning under ⅜in (1cm). Stitch along the fold and then again, about 3in (7.5cm) higher, in order to make a case for the pole to slide through; the exact measurement will depend on the circumference of the pole.

■ If the tapes need to have separate loops or rings fitted, do this now, positioning the first row of rings ¾in (2cm) from the hem edge. Thread cords as for Roman blinds, starting at one side of the blind and taking them through the eyelets on the track.

■ Attach a cleat to the window frame on the opposite side, where the cords will emerge. Bunch and knot the cords, trimming the ends parallel with the window sill. Thread on a drop weight and tie in a firm knot.

■ Pull up the blind into ruched swags at the base until it is the required length. Some ruching should remain at the bottom even when the blind is lowered.

## MAKING AN AUSTRIAN BLIND

**1** Attach looped tapes, starting 1¼in (3cm) from the bottom and 4in (10cm) in from the hemmed edges.

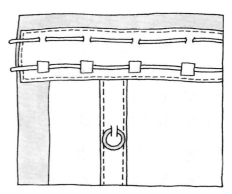

**2** Turn down the top edge of the blind ⅜in (1cm) and attach the Austrian blind heading tape. Fit with curtain hooks.

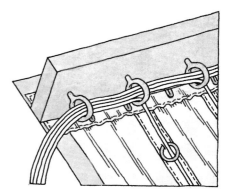

**3** Thread each cord through its row of rings and through all track "eyes," starting on the left side. Gather the cords together for pulling up the blind and knot.

# Making cushions

The cushions that will usefully and decoratively find a place in a child's room include simple cushions for piling on a bed or sofa, large bean bags for sitting and reclining (and probably jumping) on, and floor cushions for casual seating.

Cushion covers should be easily removable and washable if possible, though some heavyweight fabrics sensible for cushions which take a lot of use, such as corduroy and furnishing velvet, may have to be dry cleaned in the long run. In the short run, spraying them with a dirt and liquid repellent will help.

If the fabric has a large or distinctive design, with figures or clear shapes on it, center the pattern before cutting out so that the finished cushion has the design motif centrally placed.

## Square cushion

To make a plump, firm cushion, aim for a cover the same size or slightly

*Cushions are a very satisfying finishing touch when made to suit a color scheme or to go with a favorite toy.*

smaller than the cushion pad. For a somewhat flatter cushion, perhaps with a flat edge frill, make the cover a little larger. But bear in mind that a too-large cover will resemble a pillowcase.

Measure the cushion pad and cut two squares of material the same size, or slightly smaller, plus a seam allowance of 1in (2.5cm) all around.

■ Place the two pieces of fabric right sides together. Pin, baste and stitch around three sides. For square corners, stitch up to the seam allowance on a corner, then, with the needle in the fabric, lift the presser foot, turn the fabric 90°, lower the presser foot and continue stitching, taking the same allowance, to the next corner.

■ On the last side, stitch around the corners and approximately 2in (5cm) in from each corner, leaving an opening in the seam.

■ Clip the corners, press open the seams, press under the seam allowance on the open edge, and turn the cover right side out.

■ If you want to do without a fastener, simply insert the cushion pad into the

cover, pushing it well into the corners; slipstitch along the open edge to close.

■ To make a more easily removable cover, you can use a zipper, strong snap fasteners, or Velcro. The cover will need to be a little larger than the cushion pad if you use snap fasteners, otherwise the cushion will pop them open. Fastenings should be 4in (10cm) shorter than a side of the cushion.

■ To insert a fastening, make up the cover as above. Then pin, baste and stitch the fastening in place to the seam allowance.

## MAKING A SQUARE CUSHION

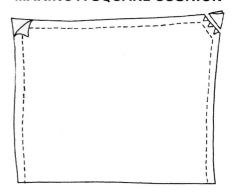

**1** Pin, baste and sew the back and front on three sides, with right sides together. Stitch 2in (5cm) along each end of the fourth side. Clip an angled corner.

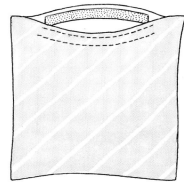

**2** Either attach Velcro to both sides of the opening, turn to right side out and insert cushion, or turn out, insert cushion and slipstitch cover to close.

■ A zipper is most conveniently fitted first, before the cover is made up. With right sides together, stitch a seam along one side, leaving an opening the length of the zipper. Press seam allowances open and slipstitch the opening from the right side. Center the zipper on the wrong side under the opening and pin and baste. With the zipper foot, stitch the zipper in place from the right side. Remove slipstitching and partly open the zipper.

■ Join the remaining three sides of the cover, as above. Open the zipper and turn right side out. Insert the cushion.

## Round cushion

The best way to achieve a perfectly round cushion is to make a simple paper pattern, using a large pair of compasses opened the radius (the distance from the exact center of the cushion to the outside edge) of the cushion pad, plus the seam allowance. Alternatively, fold a piece of paper larger than the cushion pad exactly into quarters. Tie a pencil to a piece of string, making the length of the string the same as the radius of the cushion pad, plus the seam allowance. Use a drawing pin to hold a length of string in place at the center corner of the paper.

To make a round cushion, cut a circle of fabric, plus a second circle with a slightly larger circumference to allow seam for zipper. Insert slightly opened zipper.

Draw a quarter circle on the paper. Cut around the pencil line, open out the paper, and you will have the pattern. An even simpler, though less accurate, way is to lay the cushion pad on to the paper and trace around its edge.

■ Make up the cover in the same way as for the square cushion if you are using Velcro or snap fasteners. The opening left should be one quarter of the whole cushion circle. Notch the seam allowances, press and turn. Insert the fastenings.

■ If you are using a zipper, it is best inserted into the back panel of the cover to avoid puckering. To do this, make a second paper circle and cut it in half exactly across its center. When cutting out the fabric circle, place the two pieces of pattern down with a 1¼in (3cm) gap between their long straight edges. This will be the seam allowance for the zipper. Cut out the fabric circle in two equal halves.

■ Place the two pieces, right sides together, and stitch a seam along the straight edge, leaving an opening the length of the zipper. Insert the zipper as for the square cushion and open.

■ Pin, baste and stitch around the cover, with right sides together, taking a ⅝in (1.5cm) seam. Snip into the seam allowance at intervals, and press open. Turn the cover right side out by pulling it through the open zipper.

## Piping

Piping gives a crisp look to the edge of a cushion, and can make seamlines more durable. To create a piped edge, piping cord is first covered in a length of fabric, cut on the bias; the covered cord is then inserted into the seam allowance. Piping cord comes in different weights and types, from fine to thick and synthetic or cotton. Use a piping cord that matches the type and weight of fabric you are using; if cotton piping cord is not pre-shrunk, shrink it yourself by boiling it for three minutes (make sure it is dry before use).

■ To cut fabric on the bias, fold the fabric across the grain, parallel with

the selvage. The fold line is on the bias. Strips can be cut along this line, parallel to the fold. The thicker the piping, the wider the strip will need to be, always allowing for about ⅝in (1.5cm) turnings on each edge.

■ Strips of bias-cut fabric will probably have to be joined: do this by joining the strips on the straight grain of the fabric, so that when two strips are laid right sides facing end to end, a triangle of fabric projects out on either side. Stitch ¼in (5mm) in from the ends, press flat and trim off the flaps.

■ Lay the cord along the center of the wrong side of the bias strip, fold over and pin and baste together. Stitch down the strip as close to the cord as possible (use a special piping foot attachment if your machine has one).

■ Pin, baste and stitch the piping strip to the right side of one side of the cushion cover, curving it slightly at the corners. Snip the seam allowance at the corners.

■ Continue to make the cushion in the normal way. The ends of the piping should always lie parallel to the ends of the raw fabric. If the piping cord is too short and needs to be joined, do this by untwisting strands at each end and twisting them back together. You may also need to bind over the joint.

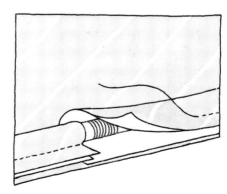

To join piping cord, unravel, trim ends to different lengths, and retwist. Cover piping in fabric, insert between front and back covers, with right sides facing, and stitch.

# Decorative techniques

## HOW TO APPLIQUÉ

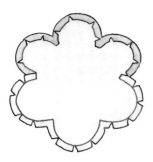

**1** Design and cut out the appliqué shape, folding and pressing a narrow hem all around, and snipping to make it lie flat. Try out the position of shapes.

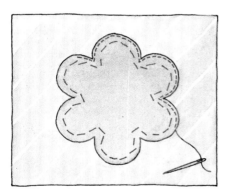

**2** Baste the appliqué shapes to the fabric in the desired position. Then hand stitch in place around the edges, taking small, neat running stitches.

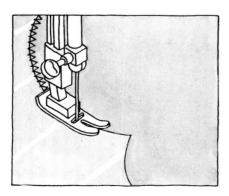

Alternatively, machine-stitch around the raw edges of the appliqué shape, using zigzag stitching to secure raw edges and prevent the fabric from fraying.

Cushions, bedspreads, crib quilts and many other items can be decoratively stitched. The techniques most readily used for children's soft furnishings are appliqué and quilting.

### Appliqué

Appliqué is the technique of decorating one fabric by stitching pieces of one or more different fabrics on to it. The pieces are sewn on to the top fabric, before you make up the item. The shapes can be carefully drawn on paper first to make an exact pattern, or they can be cut directly out of the cloth. One of the nice things about appliqué is that even quite primitive-looking, spontaneous designs have great charm. Older children can get involved with the designing and cutting out, though they will probably not be able to do any of the sewing until they are at least six years old.

Designs for appliqué can be based on anything. There are many traditional designs from all around the world, some formal, and others more random. You can look them up in design books. Alternatively, you can make up your own designs appropriate for your children. Designs can be geometric, abstract or "real." Two

simple shapes would make a tree, for example, and you could add another shape for clouds. Other suitable outlines include a clown, a rocket going to the moon, or any animal. Until you are experienced, it is better to use large simple shapes in materials that are easy to sew, such as cotton or felt, rather than small detailed shapes in thin slippery fabrics.

The material for appliqué shapes can be bought as remnants or chosen from a bag of scraps accumulated from other soft furnishing projects. Make sure the material is clean and pressed before starting. Draw the design directly on to the material in pencil and cut it out, or make a card or paper pattern first. If there is space for a large appliqué, you might find it helpful to draw the design on graph paper to get the proportions right, then scale it up for the actual pattern pieces. The grain of the appliqué piece should run

*Appliquéed cushions can be used to echo a theme elsewhere in the room. The simplistic nature of this kind of decoration is particularly appropriate to children's rooms and is not difficult to execute yourself.*

the same way as that of the base material, otherwise it will become puckered as you sew it on. Allow for a turning of ¼in (5mm) on each piece, unless you plan to sew the pieces on with a decorative edge-stitching which will cover and protect raw edges.

■ If you are hand sewing the appliqué shapes on, turn under the raw edges, then pin and baste the turnings in position. Lay the pieces on the cushion cover, quilt or bedspread, moving them around until you are happy with the composition. Pin and baste in place.

■ Use quilting thread and a thin needle for fine hand stitching, or thicker thread for hand stitching that is intended to be seen. If the stitching is to be part of the picture, you can use a contrast color, otherwise it is usual to match the color of the appliqué piece. The best hand stitches to use for hidden stitches are blind stitch, overcast stitch or small running stitch. If you wish to make a feature of the stitching you could use blanket stitch. Clever machinists can use zigzag or buttonhole stitching or an embroidery stitch to sew on the pieces; stitching will obviously be easier if the shapes are not too intricate.

■ When the pieces are sewn on, remove the basting and press on the right side, using a cloth.

■ You can make slightly padded appliqué by sewing some or all of the pieces on over thin wadding. This can be used most effectively for clouds, flowers, tree tops and so on. For a large shape, you would generally also need to sew quilting stitches across the appliqué and wadding to hold the wadding in place (see below).

## Quilting

Quilting is a technique, often used in conjunction with appliqué, that lends itself to children's soft furnishings, particularly bedding. A cover or quilt made for your baby can be just as practical and washable as the rest of the bedding, or made of more fragile materials and taken out of the crib at night or when your baby takes a nap.

To make a quilt, you sandwich wadding in between a top and bottom layer of fabric. The wadding, which can be cotton or synthetic (polyester is common), is teased out to resemble cotton wool packed in loose layers covered with paper-like material. The bottom layer is generally cotton calico or sheeting, and the top a good quality cotton, perhaps satinized. The top of the quilt could be constructed partly or entirely from patchwork or appliqué. The three layers are held together by all-over stitching which forms the quilting pattern.

To calculate the amount of fabric needed, measure the size of quilt you want and add 3in (7.5cm) all round to allow for seams and the fact that quilting draws in and so reduces the overall dimensions of the fabric. Buy the same amount of wadding. Allow for an all-around border 1¼-4in (3-10cm) wide, depending on preference, plus a narrow hem. The border could be the same or a contrasting fabric; it would look good if it were to match the fabric of any appliqué on the quilt.

■ If you plan to appliqué the top cover, do this first (see facing page). Lay the shapes on the top fabric in the desired position, then pin, baste and stitch them.

■ Then draw or trace a quilting pattern in tailor's chalk on the top fabric, working from the center out.

■ Make up the quilt by laying the wadding on the bottom fabric, right side down, and covering this with the top fabric, right side up. Pin and baste round the edges and diagonally across the center, from bottom left to top right and top left to bottom right.

■ Work the quilting, using a long machine stitch and following the tailor's chalk lines. Leave the outer edges of the quilt open.

■ To finish the outer edges, trim the wadding to ⅝in (1.5cm) larger than finished size, and the seams to 1in (2.5cm) wider. Fold the turnings inside, press flat and topstitch together.

## MAKING A QUILT

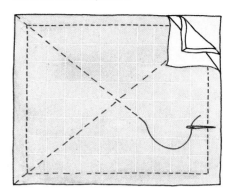

**1** Sandwich together the quilt material, wadding and lining, right sides out. Baste as shown to hold the layers together.

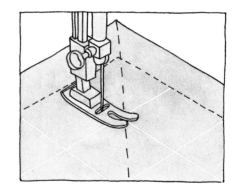

**2** The simplest quilting pattern is squares. Chalk these out in rows about 4-6in (10-15cm) apart, then stitch.

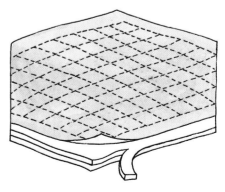

**3** Trim wadding at the hem edges all around, turn hems under, press flat and slipstitch together neatly. Attach a gathered frill or other edging if desired.

# Small soft furnishings

There are many small items that you can quite easily make for your child's room which will personalize it in some way, or create useful extra storage. Many will do both at the same time; they can be practical as well as fun.

## Drawstring bag

A drawstring bag may be made to any size: small, for little trinkets, medium-sized for pajamas or a nightgown, or large, for laundry. It can serve many other uses too: a shoe bag, a block storing bag, or a bag for transporting a doll plus its clothes.

To alter the size, reduce or increase the proportions for the bag given here in a scale of 3:2, making the finished size 12in by 8in (30cm by 20cm) for a small bag, 21in by 14in (51cm by 34cm) for a medium-sized one, 33in by 22in (84cm by 56cm) for a larger one.

Choose durable fabric such as sailcloth, strong corduroy, denim or gabardine for a heavy-duty bag; glazed cotton, chintz or ready-made quilting for a smaller one. You also need between one and three yards (meters) of a strong cotton drawstring tape, depending on the size, or you could use ribbon if the bag will only be used for something light.

Cut out the pattern on squared paper, allowing ¾in (1.5cm) extra all around for the seam allowance. Each square is the equivalent of 1¼in (3cm). Pin the pattern on the fabric, folded in half lengthwise, and cut double to give you two equal pieces. If you wish, you could appliqué a motif on the front section (a name, either of the child or of what the bag will contain, or a symbolic shape, such as bricks).

■ Place right sides of back and front together, and pin, baste and stitch a ¾in (1.5cm) seam around the two long sides and the bottom short side; leave a gap of ¾-2in (1.5-5cm) approximately 5½in (14cm) from the top of both long sides. The size of the gap will depend on the size of the bag and the width of drawstring tape that you are using. Press side seams open.

*A personalized drawstring bag can be used for all manner of children's things.*

## MAKING A DRAWSTRING BAG

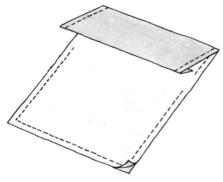

**1** With right sides together, pin and stitch the back and front around three sides. Leave a gap for the cord.

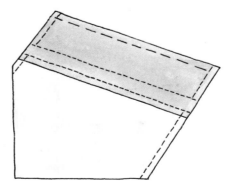

**2** Press the top edge under for a hem, then fold 3in (7.5cm) over to the wrong side of the bag. Baste and stitch the lower edge and a parallel line above.

■ Fold the top edge under ⅜in (1cm) and baste, then fold the top edge over 3in (7.5cm) to the wrong side of the bag, and baste around the top and bottom edge – part of the space in between will be the tube or casing through which the drawstrings pass.

■ Machine stitch the lower edge, then baste and stitch another row of stitches above this, leaving enough space to make a casing for the drawstrings. (It should be the same width as the gap left at each side.)

■ Turn the bag right side out. Thread two lengths of tape through the seam openings that have been left and push them along the casing, on each side. The best way to do this is to attach a large safety pin to the end of each tape and push this through the casing till you reach the exit point.

Stitch the ends of the tape together so that there is a loop at each side of the bag. The tapes will now act as a drawstring and as hanging loops.

## Hanging pocket bag

This is a simply constructed but large and lavish-looking bag with ample storage. It could initially be used to store a baby's toiletries, clothes, or soft toys; later on it might be used for books or hobby items for an older child. It is made in basic glazed cotton, and several layers of cheap lining material are used to give it a sumptuous padded feel. You could use quilted fabric, chintz or furnishing fabric, provided it is not too thick for easy machine sewing.

The sizes given below are not exact metric/imperial equivalents so it is essential to work in one or the other. It is important to keep the proportions of the bag sections even. You could of course scale up or down for a larger or smaller version.

You will need 2¼ yards (2.2 meters) of material 48in (120cm) wide, plus twice this amount of thin lining material of the same width.

■ Snip into the selvages at intervals. Cut the fabric into two rectangles measuring 72in (183cm) by 48in (120cm) and 13in (33cm) by 48in (120cm). Cut the lining, making two rectangles of each size.

■ Lay the two larger lining rectangles out flat. Place the large fabric rectangle on top, right side up. Fold the three pieces together in half lengthways, so that the lining is uppermost. Pin together along the

*A hanging pocket bag is an attractive way of storing favorite toys. It can be fixed on the back of the bedroom door.*

edges, through all layers.

■ To make the triangular flap: find the center point of the top edge and mark with a pin or chalk. Measure and mark with pins ½in (1.25cm) on either side of the center. Measure and mark with pins a point down each side, 22½in (56cm) from the top. Chalk a line from each outer center mark to the mark on each side. Cut carefully along the chalked lines.

■ Pin, baste and stitch ½in (1.25cm) around all sides and along the fold, leaving the bottom open. Press seams, trim seams and corners and turn right side out. Press.

■ Measure and mark with pins a point down each side 13in (32.5cm) from the base of the triangular flap.

■ To make the top pocket: lay the smaller fabric rectangle out flat, wrong side up. Place the two smaller lining rectangles on top.

■ Fold the fabric in half with the right side out and the lining inside. Fold and press the edges under ¼in (6mm). Stitch around the edges, close to the edge to catch the lining. Topstitch along the fold and make another line of topstitching ¼in (6mm) from the fold.

■ Place the pocket on top of the bag, matching the corners of the folded

edge of the pocket to the marks on the sides 13in (32.5cm) from the base of the triangular flap.

■ Pin, baste and stitch the sides ¼in (6mm) from the edge. Starting at the top of the pocket 12in (30cm) from the sides, stitch down the middle to the bottom of the pocket. Pin, baste and stitch across the width at the bottom to form two pockets.

■ At the bottom of the bag, fold in and press the edges under ¼in (6mm). Stitch close to the edge. Topstitch along the edge and sew another line of topstitching ¼in (6mm) from the edge.

■ Fold the bottom 24in (60cm) of the bag in half to make a third pocket across the width of the bag. Oversew the edges to the sides of the bag. Attach a large snap fastener or piece of Velcro to the middle of the top edge.

■ Attach a matching snap fastener or piece of Velcro to the inside of the point of the triangular flap and fold the flap over. Sew rings or loops on the corners and center of this fold by which to hang the bag.

■ Attach ribbons or bows made from trimmings of fabric to the pocket edges, the point of the flap and where the hanging loops are attached, if you wish to make it more decorative.

## MAKING A HANGING POCKET BAG

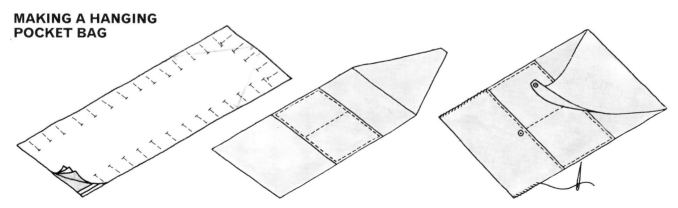

**1** Pin the fabric and lining layers together, with the folded lining uppermost, right sides together. Mark at center top and sides and joining marks.

**2** Match the corners of the pocket to the marks on the side of the bag. Stitch the sides of the pocket to the bag down the middle and across the bottom.

**3** Fold up the bottom of the bag to form a third pocket. Slipstitch the side openings. Attach Velcro or snap fasteners to the center top edge and the flap point.

# Doing repairs/1

Children don't deliberately set out to abuse their rooms. It just happens that way. Babies have toilet training accidents; toddlers wave felt tip pens around; children are sometimes sick or may scuff the paintwork.

You will obviously try to teach your children respect for property. But their room is for them to enjoy. Collect a set of basic equipment for emergency first-aid, not just for the children, but for their room. If you act as quickly as possible to clean up stains and to repair small mishaps (see chart below), you should stay ahead of the game.

If you are using a solvent, which dissolves a greasy or oily stain, lay clean cloth or kitchen paper underneath the stained layer to catch the dirt, otherwise it may spread outwards. It may in fact be better to work from the back of the stain, to push it off, rather than through, the fabric. Don't rub at stains, but dab at them, and work from the outer edge to the center. Always use a piece of clean white cloth, and change it frequently.

Most stain removers and household cleaners are dangerous, flammable and poisonous substances. Store them out of the reach of children and away from heat. When using a solvent such as acetone (non-oily nail polish remover) or dry cleaning fluid, or ammonia, make sure there is plenty of ventilation in the room. Hang any item that has been treated with a solvent outdoors to allow the fumes to evaporate.

You may, however, prefer to have as few dangerous cleaning agents as possible in a home with children, and to use only those which do not put harmful or toxic ingredients into the water supply. Safer alternatives to some of the chemical-based cleaning agents are listed below.

Glycerine can be used, neat or diluted in equal parts with warm water, to soften up many stains: this is useful if the stain is dried before you notice it. But only use glycerine on washable fabrics. Talcum powder or Fuller's Earth can be sprinkled on to greasy stains to absorb grease while you look for a solvent. Salt is effective as an emergency treatment to soak up brightly-colored spills.

## Natural alternatives

*Abrasive surface cleaner:* use half a lemon dipped in borax solution; rinse then dry.

*Ammonia:* use a mixture of vinegar, salt and water.

*Bleach:* for laundry, use sodium hexametaphosphate, diluted 1 tbsp to 1¼ gallons (5 liters) of water.

*Carpet and upholstery cleaner:* use cornflour, sprinkled over washed stain and vacuumed up.

*Disinfectant:* use borax diluted 1 level tablespoon to 2 pints (1 liter) water. But rinse well, as it bleaches quite quickly.

*Laundry detergent:* look for brands free of enzymes, chemical or optical bleaches and phosphates.

*Dishwashing detergent:* look for brands by ecological manufacturers.

## Patching up children's rooms

Remember to keep a quantity of the paint or wallpaper you used when decorating. If wallpaper needs patching, tear off (don't cut) a piece from the spare roll, and paste it over the damaged area to match the pattern.

If furniture becomes stained or scratched, it can be treated. Water or heat marks on wood can be rubbed with metal polish or car paint cleaner on a clean damp cloth, and then the wood can be repolished. Ink stains may be shifted with a denatured alcohol, but bear in mind that this will dissolve French polish too.

Scratches can be dealt with by using a mild abrasive such as metal polish, paint cleaner or a special scratch remover. If the scratch is deep, rub the wood down gently with a very fine grade of steel wool or silicon carbide paper. If the surface-protecting layer is taken off, you will have to remove it for some distance around and then apply a fresh coat.

Painted baseboards and the bottom of doors tend to become scuffed and chipped. Clean off scuff marks with hot water with a little household cleaner. Fresh dents in natural wood can sometimes be raised by making the area wet so that the grain swells up. Chips in paintwork have to be rubbed down and repainted.

## REMOVING STAINS

| Substance | Surface | Treatment |
|---|---|---|
| Epoxy resin | On carpets: | *Dab immediately with cellulose thinners or acetone for synthetic fibers, or amyl acetate for natural fibers. Once dried, impossible to remove, but try removing topmost fibers of pile plus the deposit with a sharp scalpel or razor blade.* |
| | On upholstery: | *Use cellulose thinners through fabric from wrong side.* |
| Latex adhesive | On carpets: | *Remove with damp cloth, wet the area and keep rubbing. If dried, rub with an eraser, and use dry cleaning fluid or paint brush cleaner.* |
| | On upholstery: | *As above if wet. When dry, scrape and treat with stain remover.* |

## REMOVING STAINS

| Substance | Surface | Treatment |
|---|---|---|
| Ballpoint pen | On fabric (except acetates): | Pat with tissues to soak up. Dab with a cotton ball dipped in denatured alcohol, or use a special ballpoint pen stain remover. Wash. |
| | On vinyl-coated wallpapers, toys: | Scrub at once using warm water and soap or detergent. Once the ink reacts to the plasticizers, the stain becomes permanent. |
| | On natural wood: | Try dabbing with household bleach (not rubbing, which will make a pale stain) then neutralizing with a little vinegar and water. |
| Wax crayon | On washable surface: | Wipe the surface, first with a damp cloth, then, if this doesn't work, use undiluted household cleaner. |
| | On non-washable surface: | Use a warm iron on blotting paper or paper towels over the crayon marks to draw out the grease, then dab with dry cleaning fluid. |
| | On fabric: | Dab on dry cleaning fluid or lighter fluid. |
| Felt tip pen | On carpet, upholstery and bedding: | Blot up as much as possible with cotton balls or tissues. Dab with denatured alcohol (except for materials containing acetate). Then wash using soap or soap powder or use a felt tip pen stain remover. If the felt tips are water soluble, treat with water and carpet or upholstery shampoo or detergent (fabrics only). |
| | On wall coverings: | On vinyl wall coverings use denatured alcohol or an all-purpose household cleaner or undiluted dishwashing detergent. |
| Clay | On carpets and upholstery: | Scrape off as much as you can. Dab with liquid stain remover or dry-cleaning fluid to dissolve the remains, without going through to the carpet backing. Rinse and sponge with warm water, patting dry quickly. |
| Fruit juices | On carpet: | Mop up as much as possible with paper towels and wash quickly with small amount of carpet shampoo. Or use a commercial fruit and wine stain remover, checking that it can be used on your carpet fiber. |
| | On upholstery: | Sluice and sponge with cold water, then blot dry. Or use an upholstery cleaner. |
| | On bedclothes: | Rinse under a cold tap. If the stain is stubborn, soak in weak diaper cleanser, or with a strong detergent, before washing. |
| Chewing gum | On carpets and upholstery: | First chill the area with ice cubes in a plastic bag till the gum hardens and cracks off. Dab the rest off with dry-cleaning fluid or commercial chewing gum remover. |
| | On bedclothes: | Place in freezer till the gum cracks to pieces. Then try a liquid stain remover. |
| Chocolate | On washable fabrics: | Scrape with the back of a knife blade. Soak in enzyme detergent or borax solution then wash as normal. |
| | On carpets: | Scrape off, then treat with carpet shampoo. Or use dry cleaning fluid, except for foam-backed carpets. Dried stains may respond to sponging with a borax solution. |
| | On non-washable fabrics: | Use dry cleaning fluid. |
| Finger-marks | On walls: | These can be wiped off (gently on non-washable wallpaper) with a cloth squeezed out in warm water and dishwashing liquid. |

# Doing repairs/2

## REMOVING STAINS (contd)

| Substance | Surface | Treatment |
|---|---|---|
| Milk | On carpets: | Sluice with warm water or soda water and blot up thoroughly with paper towels. Use carpet spot stain remover if necessary. |
| | On upholstery: | Sponge with warm water and blot up. If stain remains, use an appropriate stain remover or a small amount of upholstery shampoo. |
| | On bedding: | Rinse well, then wash. Soak dried stains in enzyme detergent first. |
| Blood | On bedclothes: | Dip stained area into cold salt water, then soak in an enzyme detergent. Or try a commercial blood stain remover. Dried stains can be soaked in a weak solution of hydrogen peroxide and cold water (1 part peroxide, 20vol, to 6 parts water with a tiny drop of ammonia). Don't use peroxide on nylon. |
| | On mattresses: | Tip mattress on its side and sponge with cold, salt water, then rinse. Or try upholstery cleaner. |
| | On carpets: | Sluice with cold water or soda water. Blot dry. Then try carpet shampoo. |
| | On upholstery: | Sponge with cold water plus just a few drops of ammonia. Rinse and blot dry. Or use a commercial upholstery cleaner. |
| Feces | On carpets and upholstery: | Lift off with tissue or large spoon. Sluice with clean warm water with trace of disinfectant or antiseptic. Shampoo if necessary. |
| | On bedding: | Remove any deposit by shaking into lavatory. Rinse in cold running water. Soak in enzyme solution (for white cotton, in weak diaper cleaning solution). Then wash. |
| Urine | On carpets and upholstery: | Sponge with cold water or squirt with soda water, then blot well. Rinse again with water with antiseptic added. Or sponge with carpet or upholstery shampoo and rinse with clean water. |
| | Non-washable upholstery: | Sponge with cold water, blot well. Sponge again with half a pint (300 ml) of water with 1tsp white vinegar added. Blot again. |
| | On mattresses: | Turn mattress on its side and sponge area with cold water with a little dishwashing detergent or upholstery shampoo. Rinse with water plus a trace of disinfectant or antiseptic. Blot well. |
| | On bedding: | Rinse in cold water, then wash as usual. Dried stains can be soaked in a pre-wash enzyme detergent. |
| Vomit | On carpets: | Remove as much as possible with a spoon. Sluice with water or squirt with soda water, and blot well, or rinse with borax solution (see fruit juices). Clean with carpet shampoo with a trace of antiseptic or disinfectant added. |
| | On upholstery: | Remove with a spoon. Sponge with warm water plus a few drops of ammonia. Or use upholstery cleaner. |
| | On mattresses: | Remove with a spoon, and treat as for urine. |
| | On bedding: | Shake into toilet and rinse under running cold water. Soak in enzyme detergent solution and wash as usual. |

# Index

# Index

## Acknowledgments

**Conran Octopus wish to thank the following for their help in the preparation of this book:**

**Illustrators:** John Woodcock, Katy Sleight, Will Giles, Sandra Pond

**For taking part in the photography:**
Alexander Taylor, Emily and Madeleine O'Shea, Jeffrey Sheldon, Jack Burnham, Laura and William Collins, Alastair and Julia Lott, Jamie and Emma Butcher, Robert Paveley, Katie and Joe Gordon

**For the use of their homes for photography:** Julie Taylor, Jane O'Shea, Ann Burnham

**For his work on the American edition:**
Ray Porfilio

**For painting the mural on pages 108-109:**
Maxine Cooper

**For permission to reproduce photographs:**
**1** Jean-Paul Bonhommet; **3** William Stites; **7** Jean-Paul Bonhommet; **8** Ken Kirkwood; **14** Camera Press; **18** Mike Nicholson/Elizabeth Whiting and Associates; **19** Michael Dunne/ Elizabeth Whiting and Associates; **26-7** Karen Bussolini (Architects – J.P. Franzen Associates); **37** *above* Michael Crockett/ Elizabeth Whiting and Associates; **37** *below* Colin Burnham/Conran Octopus; **41** *above* Crown Paints; **46** Jean-Paul Bonhommet; **50** La Maison de Marie Claire/Pataut/Comte; **51** Tim Woodcock; **54** Syndication International; **56** William Stites; **59** *above* Crown Relief Decorations; **59** *below* Jan Baldwin/Conran Octopus; **62** Michael Dunne/Elizabeth Whiting and Associates; **64-5** Annet Held; **65** *above* Crown Paints; **66** Syndication International; **67** Spike Powell/ Elizabeth Whiting and Associates; **86-9** William Stites; **70** Michael Dunne/Elizabeth Whiting and Associates; **72** Kingfisher Wallcoverings; **76** Jean-Paul Bonhommet; **77** Dragons of Walton Street, London; **79**

Karen Bussolini (Architects – J.P. Franzen Associates); **80-1** La Maison de Marie Claire/ Girardeau/Postic; **81** *above* La Maison de MarieClaire/Bestel/Pascal; **83** Spike Powell/ Elizabeth Whiting and Associates; **84** La Maison de Marie Claire/Pataut/Comte; **85** La Maison de Marie Claire/Scotto/Puech; **86** Boys Syndication; **89** *below* Annet Held; **90** Jean-Paul Bonhommet; **91** Ken Kirkwood; **101** Di Lewis/Elizabeth Whiting and Associates; **106** Jan Baldwin/Conran Octopus; **108** Arthur Sanderson and Sons, Ltd.; **111** Karen Bussolini (Designer: John Canning); **114** Kingfisher Wallcoverings; **118** Michael Crockett/Elizabeth Whiting and Associates; **126** Spike Powell/Elizabeth Whiting and Associates; **130** Tim Street-Porter/Elizabeth Whiting and Associates; **134** Jessica Strang (Designer: Chris Francis).

**For photography for Conran Octopus:**
Julie Fisher: **4-5; 10-11; 24-5; 48-9; 60-1; 116-17; 136.**
Jon Bouchier: **15; 17; 20-1; 35; 38; 41** below; **42; 45; 52; 71; 88-9; 92; 122; 132; 137.**